# MEET THE
# BEASTS

# MEET THE
# BEASTS

## FRANK MAZZAPICA

## MEET THE BEASTS:
### A Simple Guide to Identifying the Five Beasts of Revelation

RevMedia Publishing
P.O. Box 5172
Kingwood, TX 77325
www.davidyanezministries.com
www.revmediapublishing.com

ISBN: 978-0-9904764-2-9
Printed in the United States of America
© 2014 by Frank Mazzapica

1  2  3  4  5  6  7  8  9  10  11  |  21  20  19  18  17  16  15  14

# CONTENTS

Introduction ................................................................. 7

  1.  The Beast from the Waters: The Antichrist ...................... 11

  2.  The Beast from the Land: The False Prophet ................... 29

  3.  The Whore of Babylon: The Vatican and the Pope ........... 33

  4.  The Crimson-Colored Beast ........................................ 54

  5.  The Dragon Beast ....................................................... 64

  6.  The Beast out of the Abyss: Apollyon ............................. 74

Conclusion ................................................................. 84

# INTRODUCTION

This book attempts to describe, in simple terms, the five beasts identified in the book of Revelation for those readers who have no time or interest in peeling back the multiple and confusing layers of end-times clues and symbols. For many readers of the Bible, deciphering the signs and wonders, seals, and trumpets mentioned in the book of Revelation may be too exhausting to tackle.

Each chapter of this book describes one beast, using the backdrop of its respective Bible chapter. Throughout, I have also added my speculations, for whatever they are worth, as to who the five beasts are, including the Antichrist and the false prophet. Regardless of their ultimate identity, however, it is imperative that the reader recognizes that the power behind these beasts, and the evil armies of men and demons, is Satan himself.

I have designated a chapter specifically for the "whore of Babylon." And though this harlot is not included as one of the beasts of this book, I feel that it is relevant understanding who is riding the crimson beast, and why she has so much power over this beast.

It is my hope that these chapters read easily for you. You will find that I make bold and direct statements as to who the beasts are and those that are peripherally involved as agents from Satan. I must admit I was challenged to remain focused only to points that emphasize each of the beasts and his role in the plan of Satan to destroy all that is good and righteous. There are so many intriguing tangents a student or writer of eschatology could take in describing the signs and wonders of the end times. Avoiding these tangents has been my challenge. Had I thrown all caution to the wind, this book would be hundreds of pages long, and my purpose of simplicity and directness would have been lost.

The war that is now mounting and quickly approaching will be horrific. Satan will be on the earth, micro managing an attack, unlike anything we have ever seen, on God's people and mankind in general. Satan will be in a panic state, hurried and angry, because his time is running out. He will be a totally *hands-on* leader, using the five beasts and the whore of Babylon to perform huge damage and abominations before God and man. As I mention in the following chapters, there is no hope for man to stop or overcome this coming terrible onslaught of Satan without a personal rescue mission by the Son of God, Jesus the Christ. He is our only hope, and the Jews will see this and weep bitterly as they see Him coming from the clouds in His Second Coming.

The victories of these beasts may surprise the reader. Through mass deceit, new laws, and outright war, the beasts will successfully make war on the people of God for a season, and will invade Israel, putting the Jewish people to flight one more time. The coming invasion of Israel will be successful for a while. And those Christians who believe in the one true God and Jesus Christ as the only Savior, and the only way to the Father and heaven, will initially suffer greatly as well. These days will be days of sorrow and tribulation. I am not a post-tribulationist, but I am inclined to see troubles coming to the people of God before their rapture.

I do, however, believe in the symbolic *"land of Goshen"* in which the people of God will be safely harbored, covered, and protected from many of the attacks and plagues that will consume much of the earth and mankind. As a quick example, once the beast from the abyss is released for five months to torment man like a scorpion, God will instruct the demon locusts, that follow the beast out of the abyss, to not harm the people on the earth that are sealed by God. He will send an angel from heaven to divide the sheep from the goats, and the tares from the wheat. (See Matthew 3:12.)

Many writers have dismissed much of the holy writ in Revelation as mere myth, sheer symbolism, or philosophical metaphors to learn from. Sadly, many churches and seminaries around the world have summarized the Revelation of Jesus Christ and the vision of John the apostle as events of the past (historicists and preterists), and that we are not to be concerned with these signs, for they are irrelevant to our future. However, these coming events, the war that is to be waged, and the destruction that will be experienced has never happened at this terrorizing level in all of history. There is nothing to compare the coming of these five beasts, and nothing in man's past can compare to the coming battle of Armageddon or the return of Jesus Christ.

Many preachers steer clear of end time Scripture texts that may scare or challenge their congregations. There is an apprehension on some preachers' parts that it will run off the members of their churches. Preachers who tend to speak on end times are often referred as to those who concentrate on scare tactics to manipulate the people of God. I disagree with this assessment. First, because, I have recognized that the people of God are interested and intrigued with the end times. I also must proclaim that we are all to be *watchers on the wall*, warning the people of the dangers that may approach us. It is a responsibility of everyone, most certainly preachers, to be alert, sound the alarm, and *to watch and pray.*

To those who are afraid of these revelations of the beasts and the soon coming of the great and terrible day of God, I ask you to find peace and solace in knowing that this is what we have been waiting for our entire Christian lives. And though the days will be dark and fearsome, know that the intent of God is to destroy evil, to separate you from the world, and to bring you closer to Him and to our rapture. The main purpose of His fierce return is a rescue mission for us and against all that is evil. He will defeat sickness and death, and bring to judgment all that is wicked.

—*Frank Mazzapica*

# CHAPTER ONE
# The Beast Out of the Waters

# 1

# THE BEAST FROM THE WATERS: THE ANTICHRIST

**B**efore I begin to paint you a vivid picture of the Antichrist, a broader stroke of my brush requires me to define an important term called *"the spirit of antichrist."* In 1 John 4:3 (NIV), John states, *"but every spirit that does not acknowledge Jesus is not from God. This is the spirit of antichrist, which you heard is coming and now is already in the world. "*

Antichrist simply means a spirit *or* person in opposition to God. If you ever hear a person or church teach that Jesus is not the Christ, or Jesus is not the only Christ, or Jesus is not the only Son of God that came from heaven, then they are of the *spirit of antichrist,* as contrasted with the actual Antichrist. (See 1 John 2:22.) If you hear a teacher attempt to share that salvation is *also* with another Christ, he or she is of the *spirit of antichrist.* If you hear a teacher who states that Christians should have a more open or expanded mind, in that Jesus is not the only way to the Father or to heaven, and that all roads really do lead to heaven (such as the teachings of Allah, Buddha, Muhammad, Gandhi, Confucius, or of the one hundred million Hindu gods) they are of the *spirit of antichrist.*

The word antichrist is only mentioned four times in Scripture, and only by John the Beloved, in his letters of First and Second John. And those references include alluding to the *spirit of antichrist.* The *spirit of antichrist* has been in the world since the first century:

*"For many deceivers are entered into the world, who confess not that Jesus Christ is come in the flesh. This is a deceiver and an antichrist"* (2 John 1:7), meaning that men, right after the ascension of Christ, began to deny Jesus was the Christ and made themselves out to be God or the Christ.

John was inspired to alert true Christians to hold on to the original teachings of Jesus and the apostles. The spirit of antichrist does not confess the great limitations of being a human, and conversely, the antichrist doctrine refuses to confess the unlimited nature of Jesus, the only Christ and true Son of God.

+ Antichrists do not teach that Jesus came to the earth in the flesh.

+ Antichrists (according to John) have come out from us originally.

+ Antichrists do not teach that Christ literally lives within us.

+ Antichrists do not teach us that Christ was righteous in our stead.

+ Antichrists do not teach that Jesus Christ is returning to the earth.

+ Antichrists do not believe that Jesus is the only way to heaven.

+ Antichrists do not believe that Jesus is the only way to God.

As mentioned above, John tends to define an antichrist as a person(s) who comes out from the body of Christ, and then turns away from the church and Jesus. We can see this clearly in 1 John chapter two:

> Dear children, this is the last hour; and as you have heard that the antichrist is coming, even now many antichrists have come. This is how we know that this is the last hour. They went out from us, but they did not really belong to us. For if

*they had belonged to us, they would have remained with us;
but their going showed that none of them belonged to us.*

(1 John 2:18–19 NIV)

Now the actual individual, the Antichrist, is literally Satan in the flesh. (See Revelation 13:2.)

**The Antichrist is the most infamous, much heralded man-Satan that will ever pose as the Christ, or oppose God in his allegiance with Satan. He is literally a man totally possessed by Satan himself.**

The Antichrist will present himself as the almighty God. (See Revelation 13:4–5.) He has been given many titles in the Scriptures such as: the Antichrist, the Assyrian, the king of Babylon, the spoiler, the king of fierce countenance, the man of sin, the son of perdition, the wicked or (that wicked), and the beast, to name most. Everything about this man-devil will be blasphemous toward God, God's people, and God's temple. Even the Antichrist's symbolic seven heads have blasphemies toward God written all over them. (See Revelation 13:1.) When he opens his mouth to speak, he speaks with great blasphemies, even against the name of God, and those who are in heaven as well. (See Revelation 13:6.)

It is the intention of the Antichrist and Satan to humiliate and insult God through mankind. Though the Antichrist wants to physically kill the Jews and Christians, raze the land of Israel, and wipe out all infidels from the face of the earth, there is no greater contentment of the Antichrist than to blaspheme God through the mouths and actions of God's people.

The Antichrist will be immensely popular to the point of literal worship of him. People will adore everything about him, including his frequent blasphemies. As a matter of fact, his blasphemies toward God will be an alliance he will share with all those who believe and follow the Antichrist. Nearly everyone will be blaspheming God because the Antichrist is blaspheming God!

**The Antichrist is an incredible, masterful deceiver, using all sorts of deceptive words like: peace, unity, cooperation, acceptance, and promises of a safe and abundant life. (See Daniel 8:25.)**

He will be a supernaturally gifted orator. He will speak with a warm smile coupled with a determined regard to help you and your family access resources important for a good life. He will often seem stern in regard to his focused resolve to bring the world back to a balance or homeostasis. His personal presentation will have a captivating, spiritual accent as well. His words will resonate in your soul and spirit. Hollywood will adore him, as will many of your friends, relatives, neighbors, and coworkers. And if you even suggest that there's something wrong with him, or that the Holy Spirit has told you that he is not to be trusted, your friends and family may castigate you for feeling that way about him.

His wisdom will be so breathtaking that his political outreaches to kings and clerics will be irresistible. His leadership will be so awesome that many will say, "Why didn't we think of that before?" Crowds will throng to him like a John F. Kennedy on steroids. Multitudes will mob his speaking arenas, conventions, and all will huddle around the televisions as he shares his plan to rescue all of us from our plight. He will strive to blend all of our nations into one huge nation without boundaries. He will create a one-world currency along with forgiving all of our national debts toward one another. He will encourage, even direct, all religions, cults, and denominations to meld together as one.

The media will fawn over his intellect, wisdom and determined leadership. As mentioned before, he will have supernatural abilities in oration. Yes, he will be worshipped; and even if you don't, many or most of your close friends and acquaintances will.

His remedies to our political, economic, commercial, religious, agricultural, and medical needs will be exactly what we feel we all have needed all along. His authority (given to him by Satan, Revelation 13:5) will seemingly have no limits to what he can do or will want to do. He will have *carte blanche* with all of our lives, our countries, our families, and our future.

**The spirit of antichrist and his deceit will be extremely powerful– multitudes will believe him.**

Though God is restraining the Antichrist's appearance, deceit, and destruction (2 Thessalonians 2:6–7), it's going to be very difficult not to believe in his lies. The persuasion will be so incredible that it might even deceive the very elect – or more specifically— the true, God-fearing Christians.

> *For there shall arise false Christs, and false prophets, and shall shew great signs and wonders; insomuch that, if it were possible, they shall deceive the very elect.*          (Matthew 24:24)

**The Antichrist will be made boss over nearly everything and everyone. (See Revelation 13:4–5.) He will facilitate a new world order, thereby removing all national boundaries, any cultural, ethnic, or tribal diversities and consequently rule over the entire world.**

Because of his masterful deception, he will be quite irresistible to the vast majority of humans throughout the world. There will not be separate nations if the Antichrist can help it. The Antichrist will forcefully attempt to put an end to independent countries, separate currencies, and appointed leaders and armies.

Why in the world will this man-Satan remove the barrier lines between countries? First, because he will be given great authority over nearly every person on the earth, and he will be able to do whatever he wants to do for the first forty-two months of the seven-year peace treaty. (See Revelation 13:7, 5.) And second, he will have the ability to perform miraculous signs and lying wonders that will cause the people on earth to believe that he is truly God!

**He will be quick to make a covenant or a peace treaty with many nations, tribal leaders, kings, and religious leaders all over the world—in order to control the whole earth.**

He will author a dreaded peace treaty between Islam and Israel that is to last for at least seven years. Presently, we are watching the nations vigorously attempting to process a peace plan between Israel and Islam, the Palestinians, all the Muslim nations, the Vatican, and the United Nations. U.S. Secretary of State, John Kerry, who is one of the mediators of this peace pact, set a goal to complete this treaty by April 2014.

The Antichrist's offer of peace, food, water, shelter, safety, the end of wars, and the instrumentation of a fair and managed solidarity would be difficult reject. Most probably, and this is my opinion, the world will be quite ready for a drastic change after a *cataclysmic disaster* that will produce a great need to turn to a new world order just to survive.

**In fact, God will have His hand in the spreading of the delusion.**

*And for this cause God shall send them strong delusion, that they should believe a lie: That they might be damned who believed not the truth, but had pleasure in unrighteousness.*
(2 Thessalonians 2:11–12)

Right now, at the time of this writing, the lies of the spirit of antichrist are quite strong; strong enough for many people and even churches to turn to immorality; and this is during a period in which God is restraining the *spirit of antichrist*. Can you imagine the level of deception that will fill the world once the Antichrist is released among the people?

**There is no question in my mind: the Antichrist will come directly from a Muslim, radically Islamic, Middle Eastern nation, and not from Europe as some propose.**

More specifically, he will probably be from Syria (Assyria), Iran (Persia), or Iraq (Babylon). But no matter what nation he will emerge from, Iran will be the nation to recognize him, announce his arrival, present him to the world, and defend him. At the time of this writing, Iran has already chosen *the one* through self-fulfilling prophecy. It's just a matter of time for them to lift this preselected, satanic Antichrist onto his prophetic white horse and march him and his great armies before the multitudes, in a time of great rejoicing.

The reader must keep in mind that most end time prophecies are centered on Jerusalem, Israel, Muslim nations, and more generally, the Middle East. Much of the words of prophecy do not address the influence of the Antichrist on America, Europe, or other global regions. Though the Scriptures are clear that the entire world will be affected, the vast majority of influence will be in and around Israel. Much of the rejoicing for the appearance of the Antichrist will come from the billions who adhere to the Muslim prophesies, and to those ecumenical Christians who feel it needful to merge the Bible with the Quran.

It is clear in chapter thirteen of the book of Revelation that the Antichrist is a beast that comes directly *out of the waters*— meaning right out from among the multitude of men, or amid the tempest of men. The waters or seas of mankind will be in a chaotic, desperate state, and there will be no man, elected or otherwise, who has any of the remedies necessary to rescue the world. So, up from the (troubled) waters will come forth a man so unique and powerful that he will have the answers that have evaded every one of us. But make no mistake—he is certainly the work of Satan (see Revelation 13:2), much like Jesus was the work of God. The Antichrist is nothing shy of Satan incarnate.

**The Islamic antichrist, right now, is looking to change laws and time. (See Daniel 7:25.)**

Islam has a body of laws called *sharia law*. It is a very harsh set of laws with very cruel consequences. For instance, sharia law calls for the killing of adulterers, homosexuals, Muslims who convert to Christianity, those that speak out against Islam, Muhammad, Allah, or even the Law itself. Beheading is the most accepted way to kill those who commit these infractions.

Sharia law is national law in many regions around the world and even in some democratic nations. In London, for instance, some neighborhoods are posted with sharia law observances and have Islamic law enforcements patrolling the streets. It is the desire of radical Islam to change the law of the land in all nations and institute sharia law wherever they can.

Daniel 7:25 also states that the Antichrist will seek to change time. Right now in Mecca, the Muslims built the largest outdoor clock in the entire world. Even though everyone else sets their clocks and time zones on Greenwich Mean Time, Islam seeks to change the time zones to Mecca time.

**The Antichrist will probably be from ancient Assyria; he is called the Assyrian.**

Many students, theologians, and commentators believe that Isaiah 10:5–6 describes the Antichrist coming out of ancient Assyria. Many believe that the prophet Micah is describing the Antichrist coming out of Assyria in Micah chapter five.

> *And this man shall be the peace, when the Assyrian shall come into our land: and when he shall tread in our palaces, then shall we raise against him seven shepherds, and eight principal men.* (Micah 5:5)

At one time, Assyria was a world empire with the capital being Nineveh. So, the nationality of the Antichrist being an Assyrian is difficult in that ancient Assyria is presently modern day northern Iraq, Syria, Turkey, Lebanon, and Iran, with present-day Syria bordering northern Israel.

It is quite possible for the Antichrist to come out of any of the aforementioned nations and still be considered coming "out of Assyria."

Some commentaries suggest that, according to Nahum, the Antichrist will rise out of the city of Nineveh. In the book of Nahum, Nahum the prophet prophesies directly against the city of Nineveh.

> *There is one come out of thee, that imagineth evil against the* LORD, *a wicked counselor.* (Nahum 1:11)

There are other writers who believe that the Antichrist must be of a Jewish linage, no matter the nation he comes out of—be it Syria, Turkey, or even Iran. These writers feel that the Jewish people will not trust anyone but a Hebrew to step into the temple as a leader. Many counter that a Jew would never massacre thousands of Jews, if they were his own people. But in Isaiah, it is stated that the Antichrist will kill his own people, meaning the Jewish people. (See Isaiah 14:20.)

However, no matter the specific city or even the name of a nation, I believe the Antichrist will rise out of the Islamic/Muslim masses of people (beast out of the sea) in the geographical area of present-day Middle East.

**Radical Islam is the army of the Antichrist.**

Radical Islam is a raging, death-addicted, blood thirsty, satanic killing machine led by the Antichrist.

*And in the latter time of their kingdom, when the transgressors are come to the full, a king of fierce countenance, and understanding dark sentences, shall stand up.* (Daniel 8:23)

The Antichrist will kill many people *without warning*, which suggests terrorism, which we have witnessed for many decades via radical Islam. Radical Islam has terrorized nations, cities, and public markets with suicide bombers—killing innocent men, women and children—either being the victim of a mass shooting or bombing, the victim of hostage situations, or even a massive destruction like 9-11, the Boston Marathon bombing, African mall attacks, government buildings being blown up, or even our embassies overseas being razed and our dignitaries killed and beheaded.

**The armies of the Antichrist will be made from many nations and groups—mainly Islamic nations.**

Many nations presently have great ambitions to destroy Israel and America. These nations are inclined to wiping Israel off the face of the earth. These nations and groups include: *Iran, Iraq, Syria, Turkey, Tunisia, Libya, Egypt, Somalia/Ethiopia, Lebanon, Yemen, Oman, and fierce groups like Hamas, Hezbollah, Al Qaeda, Taliban, and the Muslim Brotherhood.* Powerful nations like *Russia (Gog and Magog), China, North Korea, and even Cuba* all have their vested interests in the Middle East and will find their way to the battle of Armageddon. Incidentally, forty percent of the current Russian military consider themselves Muslim.

There are four military blocks that have different beliefs but have common interests: *the Shiite block, the pro-Muslim brotherhood block, and the Sunni block, the anti-Iranian/anti-Muslim brotherhood block,* none of which ally with Israel or the United States. Though they fight among themselves concerning theology and other religious matters, they are all on the same page when it comes to Israel. Most assuredly, these Muslim or radical Islamic nations all agree that Israel must be eliminated.

**The Antichrist's radical Islamic armies are declaring in many nations (specifically northern Africa and the Middle East) that if you do not believe in Islam, you must convert, or they will simply kill you; this is why he is referred to as the beast. (See Revelation 20:4.)**

We have seen and read in the news about the constant attacks on Christian and non-Muslim territories. In some areas, victims are given the choice: being beheaded for not being Islamic, converting to Islam, or paying a severe penalty tax.

The number of people that the Antichrist will kill is described in way of *multitudes.* The cities he will destroy and the genocides he will facilitate will be horrific. (See Daniel 8:25.) He will wage war against the multitudes of Christians and Jews, and have the power to temporarily overcome them (see Revelation 13:7), according to what God allows.

The Antichrist will defeat many nations, waging war with every ruler, power, throne, and people that stands against him—including God Himself (Revelation 13:6). Islam wages war regularly against everyone that is not like them. Islam wages war against anyone that doesn't convert to Islam, and anyone that speaks out against Islam, and anyone that converts out of Islam. Islam propagates that they are the supreme and sovereign religion of the world. Islam has killed hundreds of thousands of innocent people each year in the name of Allah. They speak great blasphemies against the true God of Abraham, Isaac, and Jacob, or, more plainly, the

Judeo-Christian God. Their motivation is based upon death to the infidels and Zion, and death to anyone who is not a radical Islamic Muslim.

There are hundreds of thousands of radical Islamists dedicated to the call of Mohammed, the Quran, Muslim prophesies, for the killing of all Jews and infidels. They are dedicated to present day Islamic prophets who herald the call of death and worldwide jihad. You can find the spread of hatred, death, torture, threats, killing, maiming, kidnapping, plotting, scheming, and beheading innocent people in every country of the world. These murderous radical Islamists claim that Allah has called them to kill in order to receive blessings for their family as well as for themselves. Suicidal bombers are highly honored and receive great ovation from their leaders. Their families are compensated once they have killed many, sacrificing their own life in the process.

These jihadists are beasts. They are the handiwork of Satan. They are motivated by hatred, revenge, and total annihilation of the people of God. The only thing worse than their murdering and torturing is their blasphemies toward the one true God.

The spearhead of this Islamic army is Iran (or ancient Persia). Iran has already announced that their messiah (Mahdi) and their concept of Jesus (Isa) has met with their religious prelates and political leaders, and is about to be revealed to the entire world, to the joy and anticipation of Muslims everywhere. This announcement was heralded via a video produced by the Iranian government that was only meant to be seen by the Iranian military members. However, the video mistakenly was released onto You Tube for the whole world to see. (You Tube release: "The Coming is Upon Us—Iran—Imam Mahdi—Messiah").

This Iranian-sponsored video presentation also encourages any viewer to assassinate the King of Saudi Arabia, King Abdullah.

And once this assassination or death occurs, the Iranian leaders guarantee the imminent reappearance of Mahdi.

**The Iranian government is bent on ushering in the Mahdi (their messiah)—or to us—(the Antichrist) as soon as possible.**

The Iranian clerics have proclaimed that they must first build up a great army, campaign for the destruction of Israel, and establish the sovereignty of Islam before their messiah will come. This position motivates the Islamic world to join in the destruction of Israel, America, and democratic nations like Great Britain, to assist with the speedy arrival of their messiah. The means by which Iran has chosen to spread Islam is by infiltrating nations with warfare, weapons, and insurrection, overthrow governments, create rebellions, fund anti-Semitic campaigns, propaganda, education, bribes and negotiating, or just plain trouble making. They covertly smuggle weapons into nations that are fighting, finance the making of nuclear capability, and spread hatred, fear and death, while building alliances with evil despots throughout the world.

Iranian leaders have announced their messiah (Mahdi) is bringing peace very soon, and that their "jesus" (Isa) will renounce Judaism and Christianity. Iranian clerics continue to prophesy that their Isa will proclaim that Islam is the sovereign religion. This lying and self-fulfilling prophecy, as I have said, has stirred frenzy and encouragement among the warmongering jihadists to terrorize and kill Jews and Americans worldwide so that they may see their long-awaited Mahdi.

**The Antichrist will stop the Jews from offering sacrifices and put some abominable symbol in the rebuilt temple.**

> …*he shall cause the sacrifice and the oblation to cease, and for the overspreading of abominations he will make it desolate,*

*even until the consummation, and that determined shall be poured upon the desolate.* (Daniel 9:27)

If, per chance, the Vatican builds the third temple, and initially permits the Jews to offer sacrifices to God, it will be just a matter of time until the Vatican will disallow the sacrificial rituals to continue. The false prophet, (introduced in chapter two), could very much come out of the Vatican (meaning the pope), and if that is the case, the pope will demand complete control of Jerusalem, the temple mount and the temple, and place the Antichrist on the throne in the temple. Actually, once the temple has been secured from the Jews, the United Nations, and the United States, the Antichrist will present himself as a symbol of worship within the temple walls on a throne constructed for his honor. (See 2 Thessalonians 2:4.)

There is no question that the Vatican is interested in the temple.

I believe that the Vatican has ambitious intentions of making this peace treaty in order to gain control of the old City of Jerusalem, and, more importantly, the temple mount, in order to rebuild the temple.

The Vatican has had plans for many decades to build the third temple on the temple site, and to establish their Catholic throne there as the second Vatican. At the time of this writing, the pope and the Vatican, Shimon Peres of Israel, U.S. Secretary of State John Kerry, and the United Nations are trying to forge this peace accord. Secretary Kerry announced that a planned treaty was to be set in place by April 2014. However, the present condition of the treaty was found to be so adverse toward Israel, that President Obama has rejected the plan with hopes that a new deal can be cut soon.

**The Antichrist and his Islamic armies will destroy both the city of Jerusalem and the rebuilt temple.**

> *...and the people of the prince [Antichrist] that shall come*
> *shall destroy the city and the sanctuary; and the end thereof*
> *shall be with a flood, and unto the end of the war desolations*
> *are determined.* (Daniel 9:26)

I realize that according to the historicist doctrine, the destruction of the temple happened in 70 AD by the Roman army under Titus. However, I believe that Daniel is referring to a third temple and its destruction once again. It will be destroyed by the Antichrist, along with the city of Jerusalem, for its final time.

**The Antichrist will even turn his armies literally against Jesus Christ as he sees His second coming:**

Daniel 8:25 is an Old Testament Scripture giving an account of the Antichrist waging war against Jesus Christ:

> *And through his policy also he shall cause craft to prosper in*
> *his hand; and he shall magnify himself in his heart, and by*
> *peace shall destroy many:* **he shall also stand up against the**
> **Prince of princes; but he shall be broken without hand.**
> (Daniel 8:25)

Revelation 19:19 is a New Testament Scripture that gives an accounting of the Antichrist and his armies waging an offensive war against Jesus Christ:

> *And I saw the beast, and the kings of the earth, and their*
> *armies, gathered together* **to make war against him that sat**
> **on the horse, and against his army.** (Revelation 19:19)

Once the treaty has expired forty-two months, the Antichrist will show his true satanic self. He will begin to speak out blasphemies to and about God. (See Revelation 13:5–6.) He will say that he is the true god, and that the Judeo-Christian God is bogus. (See

Daniel 11:36–38.) By way of definition, any man proclaiming to be God, or claiming to be the only true Christ, or insulting God with perverseness, is blasphemous.

As the season of the Antichrist comes to a close during the second half of the seven-year peace plan, he will declare a no-holds-barred, all-out war, torture, terror, persecution, and imprisonment of the true Christians and, of course, all of the Jewish people. And initially, he will be quite successful in overtaking the people of God through beheading, maiming, and killing. The Antichrist will prevail against Christians and Jews for a short season (see Daniel 7:19–21), but in the end, Jesus Christ Himself will kill the Antichrist merely by the splendor of His coming and by the breath of His mouth (see 2 Thessalonians 2:8). The followers of the Antichrist will face a very fearsome judgment as well. (See 2 Thessalonians 2:10–12.) However, this treaty, whenever it is forged, as I've said, will not survive those seven years, because he will transform from a peaceful, loving man to an aggressive and warlike beast forty-two months into the treaty. (See Daniel 9:27.)

**The punishment of the Antichrist shall be severely dealt by God Himself.**

In the end, God will take the Antichrist and false prophet and throw them into the lake of fire. The lake of fire is the final destination of Satan, the false prophet, the Antichrist, and the wicked that have lived and died upon the earth. Hell, though it has three different definitions, is actually the jailhouse of the Lake of Fire, just as paradise is the waiting place of heaven's New Jerusalem. (See Luke 16.) Satan, that old dragon, will be arrested in chains, and Michael the Archangel, as commanded by God, will cast Satan into the bottomless pit where he will fall for one thousand years.

*And the beast [Antichrist] was taken, and with him the false prophet that wrought miracles before him, with which he deceived them that had received the mark of the beast [Antichrist's mark], and them that worshipped his image. These both were cast alive into the lake of fire burning with brimstone. And the remnant were slain with the sword of him that sat upon the horse [Jesus Christ], which sword proceeded out of his mouth [killing all just by speaking]: and all the fowls were filled with their flesh.*        (Revelation 19:20–21)

The following Scriptures are believed to be a description of the Assyrian (the Antichrist and his Islamic armies) temporarily invading Israel. It is believed that shortly after this, God will crush the Antichrist and his armies.

*O Assyrian, the rod of mine anger, and the staff in their hand is mine indignation. I will send him against an hypercritical nation, and against the people of my wrath will I give him a charge, to take the spoil, and to take the prey, and to tread them down like the mire of the streets.*        (Isaiah 10:5–6).

Also, Syria is based directly north. It is believed that Isaiah, in the following three Scripture settings, is describing the crushing and defeating of the Assyrian and all of his Islamic hordes on his holy mountain and in the city of Jerusalem.

*Wherefore it shall come to pass, that when the Lord hath performed his whole work upon mount Zion and on Jerusalem, I will punish the fruit of the stout heart of the king of Assyria, and the glory of his high looks.*        (Isaiah 10:12)

*I will break the Assyrian in my land, and upon my mountains tread him under foot: then shall his yoke depart from off them, and his burden depart from off their shoulders.*

(Isaiah 14:25)

*For through the voice of the LORD shall the Assyrian be*
*beaten down, which smote with a rod.*        (Isaiah 30:31)

## Three ways in which the Lord will destroy the Antichrist's armies:

And this devastation of the Antichrist's armies will take place during the battle of Armageddon, in the valley of Jezreel. And the entire battle will take place in only one full day. This battle will all be over that very evening it started, and only one-sixth of all the enemy's armies will survive. (See Ezekiel 39:2.)

The Lord shall kill the Antichrist's armies:

1. By a plague causing their flesh to be consumed while they stand upon their feet. Their eyes will be consumed in their sockets, and their tongues will consume away in their mouths. (See Zechariah 14:12.) A great tumult will be among them and they will begin to destroy one another (see Zechariah 14:12), and this shall happen to both men and beasts (see Zechariah 14:15). The Jewish army will rise up and destroy many of them.

2. Concerning the Jewish army that will rise up out of Judah, governors will lead the Jewish army into battle and kill many. The governors are chosen because they live in Jerusalem; they have faith that God will head the Jewish armies up to victory. These governors are compared to a torch of fire in a sheaf of wheat. They shall devour and kill all the enemy armies round about, on the left and right. (See Zechariah 12:5–6.) God's supernatural defense of Jerusalem and the Jews will be so terrible that all nations fighting against the Jews will tremble and shake for fear of the Lord who will be visible over Israel.

CHAPTER TWO

# The Beast Out of the Land

# 2

# THE BEAST FROM THE LAND: THE FALSE PROPHET

*And I besought the other angel that he should show me the might of **those monsters**, how they were parted on one day and cast, the one into the abysses of the sea, and the other unto dry land of the wilderness. And he said to me: Thou son of man, herein thou seek to know what is hidden.*

(1 Enoch 60:9–10)

The false prophet will come after the first beast (the Antichrist). (See Revelation 13:12.)

The false prophet will be the Antichrist's prophet. (See Revelation 13:12; 16:13.)

The false prophet's false religion will center on the Antichrist. (See Revelation 13:12.)

The false prophet will have all of the powers, authority, and wonders that the Antichrist exercises, but the false prophet will perform all of his miracles on the behalf of the Antichrist. (See Revelation 13:11–12.)

The false prophet will be given great and amazing abilities to perform miracles and great wonders. He will even have the ability to bring fire down from the sky. (See Revelation 13:13.)

His miraculous signs will not be from God, but an evil ability that will lure many nations into lying wonders. (See 2 Thessalonians 2:9.)

The reason the false prophet will perform miracles will be to deceive the whole world and point or encourage all of mankind to look at the Antichrist as literally God on earth. (See Revelation 13:14.)

**The false prophet** will have an image or symbol created that represents the Antichrist. This image, statue, or symbol will be a point of worship for all mankind. (See Revelation 13:14.) The false prophet will have mankind create an image, symbol, statue or point of worship and miraculously cause the symbol to speak and do personal acts. (See Revelation 13:15.)

Though the **false prophet** will initially appear to be a good and kind prophet, he will become increasingly aggressive and forceful on all of mankind. Revelation 13:11 says, *"And I beheld another beast coming up out of the earth; and **he had two horns like a lamb**, and he spake as a dragon."* This false prophet will appear as a lamb initially, and then begin to speak like a dragon.

**The false prophet** will have the ability to send demon spirits, working through ambassadors, presidents, kings, prime ministers, tribal leaders, dictators, and despots, to gather the nations to Armageddon. (See Revelation 16:13–16.)

> *And I saw three unclean spirits like frogs come out of the mouth of the dragon, and out of the mouth of the false prophet. For they are the spirits of devils, working miracles, which go forth unto the kings of the earth and of the whole world, to gather them to battle of the great day of God Almighty.*
> (Revelation 16:13–14)

## 666 Symbol

The false prophet will demand, by a new law, that every man, woman, and child throughout the world receive a type of symbol that appears to be the numbers 666. (See Revelation 13:18.) Many commentaries insist that the symbol 666 is actually the Islamic symbol that appears on their flag, their kerchiefs, facemasks, head-dresses, wristband wraps, etc., and will be displayed in the temple.

I believe the 666 symbol represents a religious symbol, not one of finance. It is inconceivable that God would condemn to hell everyone who accepts such a symbol, unless it represented a devotion to and acceptance of the Antichrist. I realize all the financial ramifications the 666 symbol will have. Giving everyone that wears it (on their right hand or forehead) the ability to buy and sell—and those that do not accept the mark cannot purchase or sell. (See Revelation 13:17.) And although I accept the idea that the symbol will control the finances for everyone worldwide, the symbol is much more than financial. It is an image of the Antichrist and all the abominations and blasphemies against God and His name that the image represents.

Many believe that the 666 symbol will be a financial symbol that may appear as a capsule injected into your skin in order for financial institutions to scan. Others believe that the symbol will appear as a micro-tattoo that will give the scanner all of your personal information. Whatever the mode, the basic premise is to replace all cash, plastic cards, checks, social security cards, passports, electronic funds transfers, billing, debits and credits online, and such.

Many believe that the European Common Market, the European Union and the European financial system will create a worldwide monetary process that will control the all finances. I do not believe that Europe will devise a worldwide monetary system outside of the powers of Islam. As I mentioned, the mark of the beast (666) will be a religious symbol that demands that everyone literally worships it. Much of Europe, especially London, is eaten alive with radical Islam, as are forty percent of Russia's armies. So I must continue to insist that we all keep our focus on the Middle Eastern influence, specifically Islamic and Muslim.

If you are found not receiving this 666 symbol on your right hand or forehead, you will be killed–most likely beheaded. (See Revelation 13:15.) And if you do receive this 666 mark or symbol, you will be cast into the lake of fire.

The false prophet, the Antichrist, and the radical-Islamic armies of the beasts will actually attack Jesus Christ during the battle of Armageddon. (See Revelation 17:14.) Eventually, the false prophet will be taken with the Antichrist at Armageddon and be cast alive in the lake of fire. (See Revelation 19:20.)

## CHAPTER THREE
# The Whore of Babylon

# 3

# THE WHORE OF BABYLON: THE VATICAN AND THE POPE

**A**s you will see in this chapter, I clearly identify the papal position and the Vatican as the whore of Babylon riding on the crimson beast as described in chapter 17 of the book of Revelation. And although I do not believe that the pope is either the actual Antichrist or the false prophet, I do believe that the pope and Vatican represent a blasphemous antichrist ideology that will assemble a united, worldwide religion for the false prophet and Antichrist that will come out of the Middle East.

I realize that many people agree with this position, including commentators and reformers such as Martin Luther, who said, "I feel much freer now that I am certain that the pope is the Antichrist."

I believe that the pope is not the false prophet or the Antichrist. First, because the Antichrist will destroy the Vatican, Rome, and the papal position. (See Revelation 17:16.) And second, I believe that God Himself will destroy the Antichrist and the false prophet at the battle of Armageddon location. (See Isaiah 14:25; 30:31.) They will eventually be escorted to the Lake of Fire as witnessed before all of mankind and the angels.

**When the Bible mentions "Babylon" in Revelation, it is referring to the Vatican in Rome.**

Rome sits on seven hills, just as the symbolic Babylon is described in Revelation 17:9.

+ In the Apocalypse of Baruch 2:1, and Esdras 3:1, *Babylon* was an interchangeable word for Rome.

+ "The beast stands for the Roman empire." *Expositor's Bible Commentary*

+ "Babylon *represents Rome*" *Expositor's Bible Commentary*

**The Vatican, (the pope and Catholic prelates) is the beast of Revelation 17.**

*The woman was arrayed in purple and scarlet colour, and decked with gold and precious stones and pearls, having a golden cup in her hand full of abominations and filthiness of her fornication.* (Revelation 17:4)

This woman who is referred to as mystery Babylon (see Revelation 17:5) is wearing exotic clothing just like the priests, cardinals, bishops, arch bishops, and the have been wearing for centuries. The Catholic clergy and prelates also are known for holding golden chalices as depicted in verse four. Their vestures are made of purple and red silk with gold chains, gold crosses, gold crucifixes, and precious stones placed in them such as emeralds and rubies. Most of the Catholic hierarchy wear large gold rings and carry golden staffs as well.

You will note also that the woman displays words written upon her head that indicates abominations. (See Revelation 17:5.) The pope's hat has embroidered Latin words, which state: *Vicarius Filii Dei*, which means, "The Representative of the Son of God." This, of course, is blasphemy.

You will find that the pope's hat is also an abomination because its shape resembles the false god Dagon. The pope's hat, as well as those of the bishops and cardinals, is in the shape of an opened-mouthed fish head. The fish head also has streams of silk, running from the back of the hat and down the back of the pope, which resembles the rest of the fish's body and fins. Not only does it stand for the fish god, but the priests of Dagon wore similar fish hats as well many centuries ago as depicted from ancient etchings.

**Why is the Vatican considered the "whore"?**

The Vatican has always played the harlot with all the nations, kings, and rulers of the earth. They have cleaved to the world, loved the world, delighted in the world's riches, and has historically cleaved to wealth, gold, silver, expensive raiment, from every nation on earth. (This depicts the multi-colored beast of many skin colors and cultures). Many of the design elements included in the outfits of the Pope, bishops, and cardinals were purposely mimicked after the exquisite design of the Roman elite. The Roman dignitaries and hierarchy wore elaborate silks, robes, capes, gold, precious stones, and bright colors, such as red and purple. The Catholic clergy wined and dined with these beautifully dressed Romans and other European leaders during the Dark Ages.

It is not a secret that the priests of the Catholic Church around the world have a long history of fornications, rapes, molestations, pedophilia, secret marriages, and perversions. For centuries, many of the bishops and prelates engaged in lewd sexual practices, often secretly married, having children, selling Vatican level clergy positions for large sums of money, and presenting themselves to the people all over the world as someone to be admired and worshipped.

## The Pope

The pope, for centuries, has been presented to the world as the literal Christ on earth. He is considered holy, infallible, incapable of making an error, irrefutable, of the apostolic linage of the apostle Peter, and his words are not to be debated. Since the Vatican is an official nation, the pope is legitimately the king of the Roman Catholic empire. The pope is a very powerful man throughout the world, for he carries much influence.

+ The Vatican presents the pope as the "true vicar of Christ," according to the Vatican I.

+ *Vicar* means "stands in the stead of Christ." In other words, the pope is as the Christ—savior on earth, according to the Vatican.

+ According to the Vatican, Jesus Christ has given full power to the pope over the whole church. He is just as the divine redeemer.

+ The pope has been granted all authority of the Christ to tend, rule, and govern the universal church (Vatican I).

+ The Vatican has stated that the pope is infallible—he cannot make a mistake.

The Vatican has proclaimed the following abominations in Vatican I and II:

+ The pope defines all faith and morals

+ The pope's decisions are irreformible (they can't be changed).

+ The pope's words are Scripture

+ The Vatican has pronounced that you are cursed if you contradict the pope.

## The strength of the Vatican:

+ The Vatican is a legitimate nation on its own.

+ The wealth of the Vatican has been found to be incalculable.

+ The Vatican rules over one-sixth of the world's population and has ambassadors in 180 nations, and has churches in every country of the world.

+ The Vatican wants to remove the negative connotations of the term "Catholic" from the church in order to strengthen her grip on public affairs, geopolitics, wealth, and increased followers. It's not that the Vatican intends to rename her denomination as much as she is involved in a fresh marketing, packaging, and branding of the Roman Catholic Church in order to become more presentable, inclusive, accepting, and less stringent on old musty Catholic credos.

**According to Revelation 17:6, the woman who sits upon this beast (Whore) drinks the blood (kills) of the saints of the living God, and with the blood of the martyrs of Jesus.**

The Vatican has killed many millions of innocent people in God's name. In fact, the Roman Catholic Church, during the era of Inquisition, murdered between fifty to seventy-five million people in God's name. The Roman Catholic Church has been the most persecuting faith the world has ever seen. The Vatican throne has imposed Catholicism upon all of her subjects. "Pope Innocent the III murdered far more Christians in one afternoon than any Roman Emperor did in his entire reign" (Chuck Missler).

+ Will Durant wrote, "Compared with the persecution of heresy [by the Catholic Church Inquisition] in Europe from 1227–1492, the persecution of Christians by Romans in the first three centuries after Christ was a mild and humane procedure."

+ "The Great Inquisition of the Roman Catholic Church should rank as the deadliest blots on the record of mankind, revealing a ferocity unknown to any beast."

—Dave Hunt, *A Woman Rides the Beast*

**A few insightful blasphemies of the Vatican:**

A blasphemy, among other things, describes someone who proclaims himself or herself as God, Jesus Christ, or the incarnation of the Godhead. Popes of the past have described the papacy as literally being Jesus Christ in the flesh. The vatican does not speak of the pope as a symbolic Christ but the very Christ himself. This of course is blasphemous.

- "The pope is not simply the representative of Jesus Christ: On the contrary, he is Jesus Christ himself, under the veil of the flesh, and who by means of being common to humanity continues his ministry among men."
  —Pope Pius X (August 4, 1902–August 20, 1914)
- "The pope is considered the man on earth who represents the Son of God, who 'takes the place' of the second person of the omnipotent God of the trinity."
  —John Paul II (October 16, 1978–April 2, 2005)
- "The pope will not let Christians be saved without his authority."  —*Smalcald Articles* (1537)

**The Vatican's perceived world powers:**

The Catholic Church, at one point in history, owned two-thirds of Europe, controlled most of the nations in Europe, and had selected and dethroned leaders all over the world. The Vatican still believes that it is the epicenter of world religion.

- "Papal superiority should trump the powers of world councils and kings and nations" (Vatican I).
- "The Vatican believes that no government can be wise, just, efficient or durable for the world community without the Catholic Church and without the papacy there can be no Catholic Church" (Vatican I ).

The Vatican became like the heathen around her, and began to set up the images of her saints and martyrs, till at last, after years of gradual declension, the Church of Rome ceased to be the church of Christ; and…became the Antichrist.                    —Charles Spurgeon

### The Vatican has been anti-Semitic for centuries.

I mention that the Vatican is an anti-Semitic nation because it shows that this Vatican/beast has hated and will continue to hate and kill the Jews. "The constant inclination of opposing, attacking, plotting and scheming against the Jews has been the Vatican." (Thomas Horn and Chris Putnam in their book, *Petrus Romanus*). These authors also stated that the Vatican wants to control Jerusalem, the temple mount, to rebuild the temple, and to establish a *second Vatican* there.

### The Vatican wants to take over Jerusalem and the temple.

Why does the Vatican want to take over the old city of Jerusalem? Because the city is holy to Christians, Muslims, and Jews, and each of these religions want control of this site. Why does the Vatican want control over the temple mount? It is a most holy place to the Christians, Muslims and Jews, because the site represents the top of the mount (Dome is over this holy rock—thus called the Dome of the Rock), which Abraham stood on as he nearly sacrificed his son Isaac. Abraham is the patriarch of all three religions—Christians, Muslims, and Jews.

More critical to the books of Revelation and Daniel, this future temple sight (this will be the third holy temple built on this site—Solomon's, the rebuilt temple as described in Nehemiah; Herod's temple built during the time of Jesus Christ; and lastly there will be a modern-day rebuilt temple in which the Antichrist will reign) is very important to the Vatican, because they want to rebuild the temple in order reign from it.

Seemingly, all three religions have shown confidence in giving this holy site to the Vatican, for a few reasons. First, the Vatican presently controls several holy sites in Jerusalem, and has maintained the sites in excellent condition. Second, the Vatican is considered neutral auspices—not forbidding any of the three religions access to any of the sites. Third, each of the three religions would rather the Vatican have control of these sites in order to keep it out of the hands of the Muslims or Israel.

Lastly, there already have been agreements made in the past twelve years to give control to the Vatican, and I wouldn't be surprised to see an accord established by each of these religions to make these agreements official.

Once the Vatican has control over the temple mount, they will orchestrate the building of the temple, which will initiate great joy among Jews and Christians. The Muslims will temporarily tolerate this rebuilding of the temple on the temple mount, adjacent to their mosque, as long as they acquire land for peace.

> **"I sit as a Queen!**
> **I rule over my kingdom with great dominion and glory.**
> **I am not a widow:**
> **I am not destitute of glorious bishops and kings."**

Sadly, President Shimon Peres of Israel, in his book *Save Israel*, promised to push for the Vatican to control the holy sites in Jerusalem including the temple mount and to give political control over Jerusalem to the United Nations. Peres believes, like many others, that the temple mount and other holy sites are in good, unbiased hands with the Vatican. ("Entrust Jerusalem to the pope!", *La Stampa*, Italian Newspaper, 1993.)

The pope would have spiritual sovereignty of the old town [Jerusalem]. —Mark Halter, French/Israeli writer

Former PLO leader Yasser Arafat agreed to create *Vatican-style sovereignty* in the old city of Jerusalem.

Even the Jerusalem mayor Teddy Kollek said, "The Israeli Government should meet the Vatican's demand to apply for special status for Jerusalem." In other words, all nations should open up a clear avenue of access for the Roman Catholic Church to take dominion over old Jerusalem and the temple mount.

**The Vatican covertly works in tandem with Islam to overthrow Israel and take Jerusalem.**

Some five hundred years after the death and ascension of Jesus Christ, the Vatican authored Muslimism, wrote the Koran, educated, and gave credit to an illiterate camel salesman named Muhammad as a scheme to kill all Jews according to Alberto Rivera, Chick Publications. The Palestinian Liberation Organization (PLO), Islamic, and Muslim states have a respectful relationship with the Vatican, and share anti-Semitic sentiments.

In the Roman Catholic Church's catechism, the church pronounces their relationship with Muslims and even includes them in the salvation plan:

The plan of salvation also includes those who acknowledge the creator, in the first place amongst whom are the Muslims. These profess to hold the faith of Abraham and together with us, they adore the one, merciful God, mankind's judge on the last day.

**The Vatican, through the Jesuits, created Islam and trained Muhammad .**

The Vatican wanted to create a messiah for the Arabs, some-one they could raise up as a great leader, a man with charisma whom they could train, and eventually unite all the non-Catholic Arabs behind him, creating a mighty army that would ultimately capture Jerusalem for the pope. In the Vatican briefing, Cardinal Bea said, as reported by Father Rivera:

> In a story told by Father Alberto Rivera, in his writings called *Cloak and Dagger*, a wealthy Arabian lady who was a faithful follower of the pope played a tremendous part in this drama. She was a widow named Khadijah. She gave her wealth to the church and retired to a convent, but she was given an assignment. She was to find a brilliant young man who could be used by the Vatican to create a new reli-gion and become the messiah for the people of Ishmael. Khadijah had a cousin named Waraquah, who was also a very faithful Roman Catholic and the Vatican placed him into a critical role as Muhammad's advisor. He had tre-mendous influence on Muhammad.

> Teachers were sent to young Muhammad and he had intensive training. Muhammad studied the works of Augustine which prepared him for his "great calling." The Vatican had Catholic Arabs across North Africa spread the story of a great one who was about to rise up among the people and be the chosen one of their God.

> While Muhammad was being prepared, he was told that his enemies were the Jews and that the only true Christians were Roman Catholic. He was taught that others calling themselves Christians were actually wicked imposters and should be destroyed. Many Muslims believed this.

> Muhammad began to receive "divine revelations" and his wife's Catholic cousin, Waraquah, helped interpret

them. From this came the Quran. In the fifth year of Muhammad's mission, persecution came against his followers because they refused to worship the idols of Kaaba.

Muhammad instructed some of them to flee to Abysinnia where Negus, the Roman Catholic king, accepted them because Muhammad's views on the Virgin Mary were so close to Roman Catholic doctrine. These Muslims received protection from the Catholic kings because of Muhammad's revelations.

Muhammad later conquered Mecca, and the Kaaba was cleared of idols. History proves that before Islam came into existence, the Sabeans in Arabia worshipped the moon-god who was married to the sun-god. They gave birth to three goddesses who were worshipped throughout the Arab world as "daughters of Allah." An idol excavated at Hazor in Palestine in the 1950s shows Allah sitting on a throne with the crescent moon on his chest.

Muhammad claimed he had a vision from Allah and was told, "You are the messenger of Allah." This began his career as the prophet and he received many messages. By the time Muhammad died, the region of Islam was exploding. The nomadic Arab tribes were joining forces in the name of Allah and his prophet Muhammad.

Some of Muhammad's writings were placed in the Quran, and others were never published. They are now in the hands of high-ranking holy men (Ayatollahs) in the Islamic faith.

The pope moved quickly and issued bulls granting the Arab generals permission to invade and conquer all nations of northern Africa. The Vatican helped finance the building of these massive Islamic armies in exchange for three favors:

1. To eliminate Jews and Christians (true believers, which they call infidels).

2. To protect the Augustinian Monks and Roman Catholics.

3. To conquer Jerusalem for "his holiness" in the Vatican.

Jews and true Christians were slaughtered, and Jerusalem fell into their hands. Roman Catholics were never attacked, nor were their shrines. But when the pope asked for Jerusalem, he was surprised at their denial. The Arab generals had become so strong, that they created their own plan. Under Waraquah's direction, Muhammad wrote that Abraham offered Ishmael as a sacrifice. The Bible says that Isaac was the sacrifice, but Muhammad removed Isaac's name and inserted Ishmael's name. As a result of this and Muhammad's vision, the faithful Muslims built a mosque, the Dome of the Rock, in Ishmael's honor, on the site of the Jewish temple that was destroyed in 70 A.D. This made Jerusalem the second most holy place in the Islam faith.

As a result of the Muslim revolt against the Vatican, the pope organized armies to attack Jerusalem and called them the Crusades. The Crusades lasted for centuries and eventually Jerusalem fell out of the hands of the pope. However, today, the Muslims and Catholics work strongly together in their regions of the Middle East, especially in the old city of Jerusalem. Muslims regard true believers in Christ as poison to them and their people to this day. Now there is a resurgence of energy to once again join the Muslims and Catholics in opposing the Jews and getting Jerusalem into the hands of the Vatican."

**"Modern-day Vatican" continues to plot and scheme against the Jews.**

+ The Vatican is against Israel having a standing army.

+ The Vatican only officially recognized Israel as a nation in 2008. That is sixty years after Israel became a nation.

+ The Vatican only had diplomatic relationship with Israel in 1993.

+ The Vatican is against Jews having an attachment to Jerusalem.

+ The Vatican is anti- Zionist.

+ The Vatican feels that the Jews are occupying Muslim land.

+ The Vatican views the Palestinians as the true Israel.

+ The Vatican stated in October 2010: "No promise land, no chosen people."

+ The Vatican, in April 2002, admitted that the Catholic Church sheltered terrorists.

+ The Vatican in 2005 and 2009 condemned Israeli bombing, but not Islamic bombings of Israeli land (in which the Palestinians initiated).

+ The Vatican has been silent about the Holocaust.

+ The Vatican has demanded an "international Jerusalem" for forty-eight years.

+ The current pope, Francis I from Brazil, sounds like a Marxist, calling for: social justice, charity and truth, financial and religious equality, a world team of leaders of the three religions, national debt forgiven, and a new fair and equal monetary system.

+ According to Barry Chamish, in Vatican Assassins, the Vatican owns or controls over sixty percent of Israeli holy sites.

**Islam will destroy the Vatican and the papacy.**

Though initially (and historically for that matter) Islam and the Vatican have worked together, The Antichrist and Islam will eventually turn on Rome, destroy the Vatican, and desecrate the temple:

> *And the ten horns* [**the ten Islamic nations that comprise the Antichrist's armies**] *which thou sawest upon the beast* [**Antichrist**], *these shall hate the whore* [**the Vatican and the pope**], *and shall make her desolate and naked, and shall eat her flesh, and burn her with fire. For God hath put it in their* [**Islam's ten nations with the Antichrist**] *hearts to fulfill his will, and to agree, and give their kingdom unto the beast, until the words of God shall be fulfilled. And the woman* [**Vatican—in Rome**] *which thou sawest is that great city, which reigneth over the kings of the earth.*
> (Revelation 17:16–18)

**Rome and the Vatican will be destroyed as prophesied even by Catholic prophecies:**

> "The Vatican shall be destroyed."
> —St. Malachy (1139 A.D.)

> "Rome [the Vatican] shall be desolate and destroyed."
> —Bellarmine (1542–1621)

**The following is a compilation of quotes from a variety of sources, which warn citizens and governments of the schemes and plots of the Vatican, the papacy, and the Jesuit priesthood:**

> Do you wish to excite troubles, to provoke revolution, to produce total ruin of your country? Call in the Jesuits

(the Pope's secret agency)...and build magnificent colleges for these hot-headed religionists; suffer those audacious priests in their dictatorial and dogmatic tone, to decide on affairs of State.   —Priest Antoine Arnauld (1612–1694)

See sir, from this chamber I govern not only to Paris, but to China, not only to China, but to all the world, without anyone to know how I did it.
    —Michaelangelo Tamburini, fourteenth Jesuit General,
1706–1739

In 1816, John Adams wrote to Thomas Jefferson regarding the Vatican's secret Jesuit agency:

My history of the Jesuits is not eloquently written, but supported by unquestionable authorities, is very particular and very horrible. Their restoration [the Jesuits] is indeed a step toward darkness, cruelty, perfidy, despotism, death....I do not like the appearance of the Jesuits. If ever there was a body of men who merited eternal damnation on earth and in hell, it is this society.

Napoleon Bonaparte said,

The Jesuits are a military organization, not a religious order. Their chief is a general of an army, not the father abbot of a monastery. And the aim of this organization is: POWER; Power in its most despotic exercise. Absolute power, universal power, power to control the world by the volition of a single man. Every act, every crime, however atrocious, is a meritorious work, if committed for the interest of the Society of the Jesuits, or by the order of the general.

Adolf Hitler stated,

I have learnt most of all from the Jesuit priestly order….So far, there has been nothing more imposing on earth than the hierarchical organization of the Catholic Church. A good part of that organization I have transported direct to my own party [Nazi Party]….The Catholic Church must be held up as an example…I will tell you a secret, I am founding an order ….In Himmler, I see our Jesuits.

Hitler continued, "The SS has been organized by Himmler according to the principles of the Jesuit Order. Absolute obedience was the supreme rule; every order had to be executed without comment."

The Fuhrer had come to power, thanks to the votes of the Catholic Zentrum [Center Party overseen by Jesuit Ludwig Kaas], only five years before [1933], but most of the objectives cynically revealed in *Mein Kampf* were already realized; this book…was written by the Jesuit [controlled] Father [Bernhardt] Stempfle and signed by Hitler. For…it was the Society of Jesus which perfected the famous Pan-German program as laid out in this book, and the Fuhrer endorsed it."          —Edmond Paris (1894–1970)

The Marquis de Lafayette (1757–1834) stated, "It is my opinion that if the liberties of this country—the United States of America—are destroyed, it will be by the subtlety of the Roman Catholic Jesuit priests, for they are the most crafty, dangerous enemies to civil and religious liberty. They have instigated most of the wars of Europe."

Orestes Augustus Brownson (1803–1876) stated, "Undoubtedly it is the intent of the Pope to possess this country [America]. In this intention he is aided by the Jesuits, and all the Catholic prelates and priests. If the Catholic Church becomes predominant here, Protestants will all be exterminated."

Abraham Lincoln stated,

This war [the American Civil War] would never have been possible without the sinister influence of the Jesuits. We owe it to popery that we now see our land reddened with the blood of her noblest sons. Though there were great differences of opinions between the South and the North, on the question of slavery, neither Jefferson Davis nor anyone of the leading men of the Confederacy would have dared to attack the North, had they not relied on the promises of the Jesuits, that, under the mask of democracy, the money and the arms of the Roman Catholics,... were at their disposal if they would attack us.

The Protestants of both North and South would surely unite to exterminate the priests and the Jesuits, if they could learn how priests, nuns, and the monks, which daily land on our shores, under the pretext of preaching their religion...are nothing else but the emissaries of the Pope, of Napoleon III, and other despots of Europe, to undermine our institutions, alienate the hearts of our people from our constitution and our laws, destroy our schools, and prepare a reign of anarchy here as they have done in Ireland, in Mexico, in Spain, and wherever there are people who want to be free.

Union Army General Thomas Harris (1897) stated, "The organization of the Roman Catholic hierarchy is a complete military despotism of which the Pope is the ostensible head."

Russian novelist Fyodor Dostoyevsky (1821–1881) stated, "The Jesuits...are simply the Roman army for the earthly sovereignty of the world in the future, with the Pontiff of Rome for emperor."

Charles Spurgeon (1834–1892) said, "The sooner we let certain Archbishops and Cardinals know that we are aware of the designs, and will in nothing cooperate with them the better for us and our country. Of course, we shall be howled as bigots, but we can afford to smile at that cry, when it comes from the church which invented the Inquisition, 'No peace with Rome' is the motto of reason as well as of religion."

Francis Parkman (1823–1893), the American historian stated, "The church [Catholic] to rule the world; the Pope to rule the church; the Jesuits to rule the Pope: such was and is the simple program of the Order of Jesus."

Father Jeremiah J. Crowley (1861–1927) stated, "All through the Middle Ages and the Renaissance period the popes kept Italy in turmoil and bloodshed for their own family and territorial advantages, and they kept all Europe in turmoil, for two centuries after the Reformation, - in fact, just as long as they could, - in the wars of religion....Their whole policy is based on stirring up hatred and promoting conflicts from which they hope to draw worldly advantage....Popes and their Jesuitical agents have been and are the instigators of wars, and while the world is having real pain, Rome is having champagne. How long shall the Roman Catholic hierarchy play the people for fools?"

Avro Manhattan (1914–1990) said, "No political event or circumstances can be evaluated without the knowledge of the Vatican's part in it. And no significant world situation exists in which the Vatican does not play an important explicit or implicit role."

## Pope Francis I (2014)

The present pope, the first Jesuit to be elected pontiff, at the time of this writing, has an eighty-eight percent approval rating, and the reason for Pope Francis's popularity worldwide is his seeming acceptance of all religions and creeds, and even those without a creed. Pope Francis has been quoted as saying that his goal is to unite all religions, even those that do not believe in God, Jesus, or heaven, into one body that will be a strong peaceful resource to the whole world, bringing peace and safety to all nations.

It is Pope Francis' agenda to meld all religions, creeds, beliefs, cults, and mysticism into one world religion, and that would include nonreligious people as extreme as agnosticism and atheism. On a recent video [March 2014], Pope Francis extended an invitation to charismatics, evangelicals, and Pentecostals to join with him in the "miracle of unity."

I believe that this "miracle of unity" will be the creation of a worldwide religion far from the Judeo-Christian God that we serve. Below, please find a few quotes and paraphrases of Pope Francis that define what "unity" is to him:

+ "Whether we worship at church, a synagogue, a mosque, or a mandir (Hindu temple), it doesn't matter. Whether we call God Jesus, Adonai, Allah, or Krishna, we all worship the same God of love."

+ "Even the atheists are going to heaven." You don't have to believe in God, and you don't have to believe in heaven. Once you get to heaven you can ask God for forgiveness there [paraphrased].

+ "All roads lead to the same God."

+ On the question if the church should or should not interfere with abortion laws or same-sex laws. "Who am I to judge?"

+ It is Pope Francis' intention to bring all of the world's religions under one banner, and that would include the Muslims: "Time to intensify dialogue with other religions, thinking particularly of dialogue with Islam."

# The One Worldwide Church.

Much of the worldwide unification of churches and beliefs are being organized in part by the World Council of Churches, the National Council of Churches, Interfaith Ministries, Salvation Army, United Church of Christ, Middle Eastern Council of Churches, and the Regional Council of Churches, in which the Roman Catholic Church is a member.

They call this blending of all beliefs, The United Religions Initiative (URI). It is a global agenda with commonalities as security, health, and the common good of the people and the earth. Hundreds of large organizations and denominations are members of this unification effort. The list of religions who are endorsing members is astounding.

These organizations embrace all faiths such as: Buddhists, Islamic, Agnostics, Catholics, Anglicans, Russian Orthodox, Lutherans, Methodists, Coptic, Presbyterians, Wicca (witchcraft), Church of God in Christ, Zoroastrians, Jewish, Taoism, New Age, Mormonism, and Hinduism. These organizations pray: "in the name of all that is holy." Because they do not want to offend or leave a particular religion out, they refer to the holy one as, "thy" or "thee" rather than masculine or feminine pronouns or nouns.

Their slogan is, "We are many—we are one." And those churches that do not align themselves with this worldwide initiative are marked, separated, and identified. Your organization is considered "selfish" if you don't join them.

This one world church will have cooperative programs, sharing resources, reflecting interfaith theology, recognizing a pluralistic (work with us rather than against us) ideology, building relationships with all faiths, and encourage interfaith dialogue, coexistence, common trust, communion, true peace, health for our planet, and the Golden Rule: "Treat others as we want them to treat us." This unification is being branded "a new breed of church" and "new thought religion."

It will be difficult not to align yourself with this group (URI), because they feed the hungry, take care of environmental issues, protect the poor and needy, and assist in community initiatives. If you refuse alliance with them, you may appear as a no-good separatist. But this movement erases all signs of a Judeo-Christian God, Jesus as the only Son of God, and the true Word of God.

Much of the pope's work for unity will be for use of the false prophet and Antichrist. These unified churches and beliefs will join together eventually to worship the Antichrist.

As I have stated prior, I do not believe that the pope is either the Antichrist or the false prophet. I do, however, believe that the pope is of the spirit of antichrist, he is working against Jerusalem and the people of God; he is blasphemous, and full of abominations. I also believe that he is a tool of Satan to organize and unify religious people and hand them over to the soon-appearing false prophet and Antichrist. Once again, Islam will present the Antichrist and the false prophet to the world– most probably via Iran. But assuredly, the pope and the Vatican is the whore of Babylon that sits upon the crimson beast in Revelation 17.

## CHAPTER FOUR
# The Crimson Beast

# 4

# THE
# CRIMSON-COLORED BEAST

The wild, crimson-colored beast of Revelation 17 is a depiction of the brutal, terrorizing, bloodthirsty, ten-king confederation army of radical Islam. The Vatican in Rome and the pope (the whore) sits upon this crimson-colored beast.

The ten kings mentioned in Revelation (verses 17:3, 12) are depicted as ten horns, but they are the ten nations that will emerge from Islam to kill, pillage, torture, confiscate, burn, and terrorize the entire world. The apostle John in Revelation likens them unto a crimson, blood red, wild beast.

These ten kings are not literally kings of established or recognized nations, but have the same powers of any king in the earth. (See Revelation 17:12.) They are ten selected kings in radical Islam that rule over many people throughout the world (though they do not have any land or borders). Such kings are Hamas, Taliban, Muslim Brotherhood, Al Qaeda, Hezbollah, and the Palestinian Liberation Army (PLO).

This crimson beast is being ridden by the biblical whore, (Vatican), who sits upon seven mountains (Vatican's location in Rome). There is a tentative, but reasonable amount of clandestine power and support being provided to the Islamic ten kings who are controlled from the Vatican, similar to the control the biblical whore has over the wild, crimson beast she rides. The wild beast merely tolerates the whore's leadership, funding, and resources because it is wild. The relationship is merely a means to an end for both of them. In reality, the ten-king beast hates the whore (Islam hates the Vatican).

Take a look at Revelation 17:16: *"And the ten horns which thou sawest upon the beast, these shall **hate the whore**, and shall make her desolate and naked, and shall eat her flesh, and burn her with fire."*

I believe that this describes the eventuality that Islam will have enough of the Vatican's leadership to be able to destroy her with fire and pillage the spoil.

**These two evil entities (Islam and the Vatican) tentatively need each other to achieve their objectives.**

Islam has been in the quasi-employ of the Vatican for many centuries, and continues to support their efforts to establish Islam as a sovereign state, to kill all of the Jews, to raze Israel, to take over Jerusalem, to establish sharia laws, and to kill all Christians who do not convert to Islam. The Vatican's interest is to take control over the old City Jerusalem, especially the temple mount, to unify all religions into one world religion in the name of peace and tranquility, and to establish the rebuilt temple as the second Vatican location.

The ten-king army (crimson beast) is subservient to the woman-whore, much like the European nations were during the Medieval period in which the Roman Catholic Church controlled kings and created national policies. The Vatican was powerful enough to crown kings and dethrone them. Centuries later, and certainly after the Reformation of Martin Luther, the Roman Catholic Church lost much of her power. As you will see, while reading this chapter, that the ten-king Islamic army will have had enough of the Vatican (the whore) as well, and destroy her with fire and bloodshed. The beast she rides will turn on her with a murderous rage. The whore of Babylon (Vatican) will never rule or reign with power ever again. (See Revelation 18:21.) The drunken whore that sits on this global, wild beast is likened unto a mistress that is hated by her suitor. The Vatican is the hated mistress of Islam, and this relationship will end once radical Islam attains what it is after. The crimson beast will certainly kill the whore, as Revelation states.

## The crimson beast (Islam armies) is actually right out of hell itself.

The spirits of radical Islam, and her armies and kings, are right out of the literal, bottomless pit of hell. There are evil and unclean spirits that are being released out of hell to possess radical Islamic rulers, clerics, soldiers, tribal chieftains, and peoples that have a mandate to kill indiscriminately. They are full of sin (perdition), crazed with murder, and covered by bloodshed (crimson-colored beast) to do the work of Satan.

> *The beast that thou sawest was, and is not; and* **shall ascend out of the bottomless pit,** *and go into perdition; and they that dwell on the earth shall wonder.*          (Revelation 17:8)

Islam has written laws and policies that punish heretics (those that do not adhere to Islam), they will dictate worldwide faith, police over religion and forms of worship, imprison, confiscate, torture, and put to death all who stand in their way of perpetuating their kingdom.

## The destruction of the whore (Vatican) by the crimson beast (ten-king Islamic armies) will cause the whole world to mourn over her fall.

Islam will invade the Vatican with great ferocity, kill everyone in sight, and burn down all of the Vatican buildings, priceless art, and destroy ancient scrolls, records, microfiche, books, and parchments. And this destruction, murder, and pillage will cause the whole world to mourn. God actually puts the mandate of destroying the Vatican and Rome into the heart of the crimson beast, or the ten-king Islamic armies, as seen in Revelation 17:16–17:

> *And the ten horns which thou sawest upon the beast, these shall hate the whore, and shall make her desolate and naked, and eat her flesh, and burn her with fire. For God hath put it in their hearts to fulfil his will, and to agree, and give their kingdom unto the beast, until the words of God shall be fulfilled.*

Millions of tourists visit the Vatican each year to view the beautiful displays of huge, polished marble floors and columns. And though only thirty-three percent of the world's population is Catholic, the entire world visits and stares in awe at the beauty and wealth of the Vatican. The destruction of this center of fine art will cause the multitudes to weep.

Imagine, if you will, the armies of Islam (crimson beast) attacking the Vatican (the whore), burning and destroying all of the costly artwork of Michelangelo and Leonardo Da Vinci, such as *St. Jerome in the Wilderness*. Imagine the reaction of the world when they see the Sistine Chapel burned to the ground. Consider the destruction of the *Stanze della Segnatura*, Raphael's *Madonna of Foligno*, the *Oddi Altarpiece*, and his *Transfiguration*. What of the great Basilica of Santa Maria Maggiore, or the statue of *Prima Porta Augustus*, the frescoes, the papyruses, the papal mummies, all the tapestries, the elaborate mosaics, or the fifty-four gallery museums? Try to imagine all of the robes and altar drapes of fine silk, and velvet that is set with pearls and precious stones and covered with golden embroidery. The loss of all the incalculable billions of dollars' worth of gold, diamonds, amethysts, emeralds, opals, and rubies would shock the civilized world.

Millions will weep over the loss of such a great center of art and historical archives. If the Vatican is razed, all of the precious etchings, statutes, buildings, catacombs, carved and polished marble floors and columns, the gold and precious stones and pearls will all be wasted away.

> *And the kings of the earth, who have committed fornication and lived deliciously with her, shall bewail her, and lament for her, when they shall see the smoke of her burning, Standing afar off for the fear of her torment, say, Alas, alas, that great city Babylon, that mighty city! for in one hour is thy judgment come.* (Revelation 18:9–10)

> *And cried when they saw the smoke of her burning, saying, what city is like unto this great city! And they cast dust on their heads, and cried, weeping and wailing, saying Alas, alas, that great city, wherein were made rich all that had ships in the sea by reason of her costliness! for in one hour is she made desolate.* (verses 18–19)

### Heaven's inhabitants will rejoice when the Vatican is destroyed!

While most of the civilized world will be bemoaning the sudden loss of the Vatican, all of heaven will be rejoicing over the destruction of the Roman Catholic system, the Vatican, and much of Rome.

"*Rejoice over her, thou heaven, and ye holy apostles and prophets; for God hath avenged you on her*" (Revelation 18:20).

The Vatican, the pope and the Holy See will face such a violent destruction that her demise will be forever—never to rise in power ever again.

> *And a mighty angel took up a stone like a great millstone, and cast it into the sea, saying, Thus with violence shall that great*

*city Babylon be thrown down, **and shall be found no more at
all.*** (Revelation 18:21)

**Roman Catholic prophetic writings have been preserved, stating that the Vatican and even Rome will be destroyed.**

Non-Catholic prophets and writers do not only prophesy the destruction of the Vatican and Rome. Many highly recognized Roman Catholic prelates and prophets have spoken of the coming destruction of the Vatican city. For instance:

+ In 1909, Pope Pius VII leaned back and closed his eyes. Suddenly he woke and cried out: "What I see is terrifying. Will it be myself? Will it be my successor? What is certain is that the pope will quit Rome, and in leaving the Vatican, he will have to walk over the dead bodies of his priests." —Ian R. K. Paisley, *The Jesuits*, (Belfast; Puritan Printing Co., 1968).

+ The Venerable Bartholomew Holzhauser, (17th century, Italy), prophesied that, *"Heretics and tyrants will come suddenly and expectantly; they will break into the church [Vatican]. They will enter Rome and lay Rome waste; they will burn down churches and destroy everything."*

+ The Blessed Anna-Marie Taigi, (19th century, Italy) prophesied that *"The air shall be infected by demons that will appear under all sorts of hideous forms. Religion shall be persecuted and priests massacred, churches shall be closed, but only for a short time. The Holy Father shall be obliged to leave Rome."*

## Pope Francis I and the Jesuits—2014

It's important to mention the association of Pope Francis and the Jesuit priesthood, because there needs to be a link with this present pope and a propensity to grab power, money, and land, kill people, get involved with anti-Semitic actions, and the association of the end times.

Pope Francis is the first pope to be elected from the infamous Jesuits. This is important because the Jesuits have been the murderous arm of the Vatican for centuries. The Jesuits, much like the CIA, the KGB, or even as a mercenary group of dedicated priests, have taken secret vows to perform unscrupulous tasks for the cause of the pope and Vatican that range from assassinations, mass murder, overthrowing governments, orchestrating the deaths of presidents, heads of state, and dignitaries of countries all over the world for centuries. Jesuits have been known to set up governments and religious sects, like Islam.

The Jesuits were first formed in 1534. They are a five hundred-year-old covert order, structured as a secret military operative, demanding secret oaths and complete obedience to each direct supervisor. Their fourth vow of the secret oath is to kill a heretic, which is not considered a sin or as illegal within the Jesuit order.

The infamous Borja family, specifically Francis Borja, approved the formation of the Jesuits. Borja formalized the Jesuits into the first dedicated military order of monks of the Catholic Church. In the 1500s, the Jesuits were instrumental in the development of slave trade between Africa and South America for use in the Vatican-owned gold mines.

The Jesuits had and have exclusive powers to conduct banking and commerce for the Vatican. In the 1500s, they controlled trade of spices, slaves, drugs, and plantations as the Dutch East India Company.

The Jesuits have a long history of exploiting king's plans and promoting riots and counter-movements. In 1792, for instance, the Jesuits "Reign of Terror" executed over 40,000 people, mostly without a trial, in Austria.

The Jesuits were tremendous mentors (especially Father Frans Von Papa) to Hitler, Himmler, and Joseph Stalin before and during WWII. Incredibly, Hitler wrote that the Third Reich was a Roman Catholic Church enterprise. The relationship with Pope Pius XII and Hitler was an extraordinary sharing of power, money, and land grabs.

There are presently 19,216 Jesuits that serve in 112 nations on six continents, with the largest number of members in India and the United States. At the time of this writing, the Jesuits own fifty-one percent of the Bank of America, and they gross over two hundred eighty million dollars annually.

To show you the extent of the Jesuits monetary powers, in the 1780s, La Fayette was tasked by the Jesuits to take vast gold reserves from France to America. The stolen French gold was placed in the care of the Bank of New York (founded in 1784) and the newly formed Bank of Manhattan (now JP Morgan Chase bank).

The Jesuits are feared and highly disliked by the Catholic clergy because they act much like the Third Reich and answer only to the "Black Pope" (the leader of the Jesuit order). The Jesuits do for the Vatican what the Gestapo did for the Hitler.

Pope Francis I, as a Jesuit, broke his vow whereby he swore he would never become pope, since the Jesuits have a tradition of not accepting positions in high places. It should be interesting to see how Pope Francis conducts himself with such a long history of being a Jesuit. Though he may appear to be a meek and compassionate lamb on the outside, it is unclear what he is planning on the inside. You just don't walk away from being a devoted Jesuit for several decades, making such death-defying vows, and begin to take a totally different path. It is commonly believed that the Black Pope (the Jesuit leader) rules over the entire Roman Catholic Church organization secretly, and passes down orders to the pope that sits in the Vatican.

**Catholic prophecies that believe Pope Francis is the last pope before the end of the Vatican (the rider of the crimson beast).**

Many theologians and students of prophecy have made deductions, written articles and books and made speeches in churches and symposiums, that the last pope to reign in the Vatican before its destruction will be Pope Francis I. I have researched the logic behind identifying Pope Francis I as the last pope, and I must say their research in compelling. However, I am persuaded to share with you some information that generally points to a "last Pope" that will serve before the fall of the Vatican by the crimson beast in order to stay focused on our thesis.

There are credible prophecies that have been transcribed through the centuries concerning the destruction of the Vatican when the last pope is in leadership. One Catholic prophet that lived during the twelfth century was Saint Malachy. Malachy was an Irish saint who lived from 1094 to 1148, but his revealing prophecies were only discovered in 1590. Malachy was a Medieval priest and cabbalist that had insight into popes past, present, and future. His prophecies were transcribed in a series of cryptic verses. Malachy prophesied that the last pope would bring the destruction of the Roman Catholic Church (crimson beast), who many believe to be Pope Francis I.

> In the final persecution of the Holy Roman Church, there will sit a pope. Peter the Roman, who will pasture his sheep in many tribulations, and when these things are finished, the city of seven hills will be destroyed, and the dreadful judge will judge his people. The end.
> —St. Malachy, 12th century bishop of Armagh, Ireland

The crimson beast (radical Islam and her armies) and the whore that rides the beast (Vatican) are initially inseparable. They share many of the same goals in destroying the Jews and taking

Jerusalem. However, this relationship between the crimson beast and the rider will not last very long. The crimson beast will turn against the rider, kill, and devour her because of the hatred the beast has for the rider. As mentioned earlier, the crimson beast only tolerates the rider and her covert rule. One day the beast will turn on her.

## CHAPTER FIVE
# The Red Dragon Beast

# 5

# THE DRAGON BEAST

The twelfth chapter of the book of Revelation speaks much about the dragon. The dragon beast is Satan. In fact, the dragon is mentioned as Satan, or the devil, or the serpent, thirteen times in the book of Revelation alone.

It's important to mention that the dragon is described as the color red. The literal Greek word for *red* in this context is *purrhos*, or fire-colored. Some have mistakenly defined this color of red as the color of blood. However, the proper definition here describes the red as hot, red fire, or a seething of fire out of the mouth and nostrils of the dragon.

The descriptions of the dragon (as Satan) are many: sea beast/monster, reptilian, menacing, and ravenous, demonic, snake-like beast, frightful and powerful.

+ **The dragon** is a beastly character.

+ **The old serpent** is an ancient deceiving snake from the Garden of Eden.

+ **The devil** means slanderer of God Almighty.

+ **Satan** means the adversary of God.

> *Out of his mouth go burning lamps, and sparks of fire leap out. Out of his nostrils goeth smoke, as out of a seething pot or caldron. His breath kindleth coals, and flame goeth out of his mouth.* (Job 41:19–21)

The twelfth chapter of Revelation also shows the reader how the dragon (Satan) sat ready to kill and devour the Christ Child as soon as the infant was to born.

Satan used the power of the ancient Roman office to try to kill the baby Jesus once He was born. In 37 BC, Herod the Great conquered Jerusalem with the assistance of the Roman army and became king. Herod was a ruthless, brutal, and paranoid king that Satan would use to try to kill the baby Jesus. Herod was an uncontrollable monster who had killed at least two of his own sons, a few of his ten wives, his sister, his father-in-law, his uncle, and executed some three hundred people that were presumably associated with a scheme to overthrow him. He levied heavy taxes upon the Jewish people in order to build garrisons, buildings, and monuments, including monuments commemorating him. I say all of this to show you that Herod certainly had the unscrupulous ability to kill the baby once he was born.

Because Herod ruled over the land of the Jews and was actually a Jew himself (though he was born from an Arab family), the Romans called him the King of the Jews. Once Herod found out that there was a new King of the Jews born in Bethlehem, it was viewed as an imminent threat to Herod's position. As the book of Matthew mentions, Herod found out, through the wise men (Magi), that the Christ Child was born (see Matthew 2:11), so he sought to kill the baby Jesus.

*Go and make careful search for the young child.*

(Matthew 2:8)

The writer Matthew clearly shows how the dragon of Revelation 12 sat intently waiting to devour the Child once he was born from the woman (Israel). Herod asked the Magi to report to him as soon as they found the baby's location. (See Matthew 2:7.) Eventually, Herod would realize that the wise men did not plan to return to him any news of the Child, so he became infuriated and commanded his soldiers to find the Child by killing every male-child at the age of two years old and under in the town of Bethlehem of Judea. (See Matthew 2:16.) Historians called the massacre of all the male children the "slaughter of the Innocents". Commentaries do not reveal how many children were actually killed, however, the baby Jesus was not among them. An angel of the Lord warned Mary and Joseph that danger was coming and that they should flee to Egypt with the baby until the danger passed. (See Matthew 2:13.)

Some writings have estimated that as few as twenty children were killed that day, to an incredible number of 14,000 male children killed in order to slaughter the baby Jesus. However, most writers lean toward the lesser of the two numbers due to the estimated population of Bethlehem in those days.

Herod would eventually die a horribly painful death. It was reported by Josephus that Herod died of a disease that caused breathing problems, convulsions, a rotting of his body, and worms. Once word was sent to Mary, Joseph, and Jesus, some three years later, that it was safe to return to Israel, they returned and lived in a town called Nazareth.

Rome exterminated many of the Jews and the early Christians, and the dragon continues his plans to use Rome (the Vatican) again and again to kill God's chosen people, the Jews, and Christians who do not adhere to Catholicism. Satan has had a long love affair with the Roman Catholic Church. And through the centuries, the dragon has found a comfortable home in the Vatican, by influencing and tempting Vatican leadership and prelates with power all over the world, lust, money beyond measure, to be worshipped and praised, and a thirst for the blood of the people of God.

**The dragon has historically used many nations to chase, hunt, and kill the Jews.**

Though Satan has not stopped persecuting God's people since the garden of Eden, Israel will soon experience the worst the dragon has to offer in the last days and before the Second Coming of Christ. The fury of his wrath against the Jews and the true Christians will be the Great Tribulation.

As mentioned, Satan, as the dragon, has been chasing the Jews all throughout history, and to every corner of the earth. Many nations have been used by the dragon to wipe out the Jews, such as, the Philistines, the Ammonites, the Hittites, the Edomites, the Canaanites, and many others.

Please find below a list, though not exhaustive, of the many attempts of Satan to wipe out all of Israel by using other nations throughout history:

- 587 BC — Babylon (Iraq) attacks and destroys Israel. Exterminates and enslaves the Jews unmercifully.

- 539 BC — Persia (Iran) attacks and conquers Israel.

- 331 BC — Greece conquers Israel.

- 63 BC — Rome conquers Israel.

- 66–73 AD — The Jewish-Roman wars kill one hundred thousand Jews, and enslave another one hundred thousand. The Jews are dispersed all over the world. It is illegal for Jews to live in Jerusalem. The Romans rename Israel "Palestine" to humiliate the Jews. Palestine refers to the Philistines – Israel's worst enemy.

- 400 AD — The Barbarians sack Israel.

- 1290 AD — England makes it illegal for Jews to live in their country.

- 1391 AD — France makes it illegal for Jews to live in their country.

+ 1421 AD — Austria makes it illegal for Jews to live in their country.

+ 1492 AD — Spain makes it illegal for Jews to live in their country.

+ 1940s — Nazi Germany exterminates over six million Jews during the Holocaust. .

+ 1948 — Immediately after Israel is made a nation, she is invaded by Egypt, Syria, Iraq, Jordan, and Lebanon. Israel defeats these five nations and increases their territory by fifty percent.

+ 1967 — Israel is attacked by Egypt, Jordan, and Syria. Israel defeats all three of these nations in less than one week (Six Day War). Israel destroys the air forces of Egypt, Jordan, and Syria miraculously in one day.

+ 1973 — Israel is attacked by Egypt and Syria (Yom Kippur War). Israel defeats them in three weeks.

Clearly, the dragon (Satan) has been attacking Israel all throughout history. After AD 500, the dragon has concentrated his attacks on the Jews heavily through Muslims and radical Islamists (since its inception through Muhammad). Today, the fierceness and hatred of Islam toward the Jews is so intense, that they have openly proclaimed, numerous times, their plan to wipe Israel off the face of the earth. Their hatred is demonic, literally out of the abyss from hell.

The nations that have been used by Satan (dragon) to destroy the Jews have been referred to as beasts in the Scriptures, especially in the books of Daniel and Revelation. However, during these end times, these present beasts are unlike any beast the Jews have ever had to confront. This is because Satan has come down upon the earth personally to head up the attack as the dragon. (See Revelation 12:12.) He is raging mad because he knows that his time is very short. (See Revelation 12:12.) He is staging an all-out-war with the entire world through radical Islam, and even will attack the Son of God during His Second Coming. It will take nothing less than a powerful Savior to rescue Israel from total extermination this time. They will see Jesus Christ, the Son of God, fight for their survival. Jesus Christ will save all of Israel: *"All of Israel shall be saved"* (Romans 11:26), as He returns to Jerusalem to make war with the beasts.

### The dragon fights against the Archangel Michael and the angels. Revelation 12:7-8

Incredibly, in this twelfth chapter of Revelation, John sees Satan (dragon) convincing one-third of the angels in heaven to fight with him against the other angels and even against the almighty God Himself. Satan's deception is quite extraordinary; he can deceive angels, in spite of the fact that these angels enjoy all of heaven's benefits and the glory and presence of God. But these angels choose to believe a lie and follow the dragon. Their rebellion against Michael, the heavenly host, and God, is a miserable and an immediate failure. They are defeated and cast to the earth as fallen angels and demons. In the end, it is evident that angels have the power of self-will, to choose either to do good or to do bad. In their judgment, it does not appear that the angels are extended mercy and grace as mankind is benefited.

> *And the angels who did not keep their positions of authority but abandoned their proper dwelling—these he has kept in darkness, bound with everlasting chains for judgment on the great Day.* (Jude 1:6 NIV)

### The great dragon is cast out of heaven to the earth. (Revelation 12:9)

The book of Job shows the reader that Satan had the ability to travel to heaven and stand among the angels. This opportunity ceases once God casts the dragon down to the earth. Once he is thrown to the earth, though all of heaven rejoices, an angel warns the inhabitants of the earth that Satan has come down among them having fierce wrath because he [Satan] knows his time is now very short. Notice however, that heaven is rejoicing because they do not have to contend with Satan any longer, but while heaven rejoices, earth begins to mourn, because they now have to contend with him like never before.

> *Therefore rejoice, you heavens and you who dwell in them! But woe to the earth and the sea, because the devil has gone down to you! He is filled with fury, because he knows his time is short.* (Revelation 12:12 NIV)

### The serpent (dragon) attacks the woman and opens his mouth with a flood of water. (Revelation 12:15)

The flood that gushes out of the dragon's mouth represents the various nations and masses of people that will flood in to chase and kill the Jews. The flood also represents the overwhelming persecution the Jews will experience during the Great Tribulation that is coming to them. It will be tribulation unlike anything they have ever had to confront before as the people of God. The flood also represents scattering the Jews all over the world. Sadly, there will be one more, temporary invasion of the land of Israel that will require the Jews to find hiding places for three and a half years.

### The dragon (Satan) is really angry with the woman (Israel). (See Revelation 12:16–17.)

Some commentaries have said that Satan despises God's people because he, as an angel, was required to minister and serve the people of God once they were created. Satan had a very powerful place in heaven, just beneath God Almighty. And when God created His children, Satan knew that his position in heaven was going to be beneath the people of God, requiring him to minister to them. In Satan's rebellion, not only does he refuse to honor God's people and their rightful place in the kingdom, but also he is intent to use the people to humiliate and turn from God. He uses people to commit abominations, incite rebellions against God, and spread debauchery and false religions in order to turn man away from the true God and toward false gods, religions, and doctrines of devils. Whatever the reason for Satan's anger with the people of God, he will intensify his anger and efforts with hopes to humiliate God and exterminate His people.

**The people will worship the dragon (Satan) that gave power to the beast. (See Revelation 13:4.)**

The people will worship the dragon through the beasts, not just in a civil way, but also in a religious way. The Antichrist will sit in the rebuilt temple, the false prophet will stand on his right hand side, the radical Islamists will bear his mark, and the worldwide religion will pay homage to and adore him. They will worship him by using expressions that should only to be addressed to God Almighty. They will refer to him as deity. His power of war will be so great that all will say, "Who is able to be like him?" And the dragon's power to make war will be no match for the presidents, kings, emperors, and dictators of the world, so he will tread upon the necks of those who do not give obedience, tribute, praise, and worship to him.

The dragon's ten-king Islamic army will tear through nations, including Israel, like vicious wild beasts. Their thirst for the blood of the people of God has them crazed with spirits of murder. They will not honor, not respect, nor offer recognition to anyone who is not radically Islamic. The Bible mentions that beheading will be a mode of execution in the last days. There are increasingly more beheadings, mass genocides, tortures, maiming, kidnapping, threats of terror and war put out by radical Islam than ever before. They have consistently called for worldwide jihads, increased suicide bombings, kidnappings, and overthrows of governments like Egypt, Libya, Sudan, Syria, Lebanon, and other North African nations. There are sleeper cells of radical Islam waiting impatiently in many countries to become mobilized and activated to kill – including the United States of America.

Much of the worship toward the dragon will also be through idols and statues of the beast. Sadly, it will not go well for those people who worship the dragon, the beast, or the image of the beast, especially if they take the mark of the beast. They will all be judged and thrown into the lake of fire.

> *And the third angel followed them, saying with a loud voice, If anyone worship the beast and his image, and receive his mark in his forehead, or in his hand, The same shall drink of the wine of the wrath of God, which is poured out without mixture into the cup of his indignation; and he shall be tormented with fire and brimstone in the presence of the holy angels, and in the presence of the Lamb. And the smoke of their torment ascendeth up for ever and ever; and they have no rest day or night, who worship   the beast and his image, and whosoever receiveth the mark of his name.* (Revelation 14:9–11)

## The dragon will literally attack Jesus Christ at His Second Coming.

Satan will literally attempt to overpower Jesus Christ as He returns to the earth the second time. (See Revelation 19:19.) But Jesus in all of His glory will be the only power that can stop the beasts, the demons, and Satan. The appearance of Jesus, while coming to the earth to put a stop to the dragon, will be terrifying.

*And I saw heaven opened, and behold a white horse; and he who sat upon him was called Faithful and True, and in righteousness he doth judge and make war. His eyes were as a flame of fire, and on his head were many crowns; and he had a name written, that no man knew, but he himself. And he was clothed with a vesture dipped in blood: and His name is called The Word of God....And out of his mouth goeth a sharp sword, that with it he should smite the nations: and he shall rule them with a rod of iron: and he treadeth the winepress of the fierceness and wrath of Almighty God.*
(Revelation 19:11–13, 15)

The dragon, or Satan, will attack Israel and all of mankind with everything he has in his power. He will wage war through devastating physical means with terrifying armies; he will use worldwide deception through spiritual warfare and a false religion; and he will use fallen angels, demons, and monsters that have never been seen by the world who have been imprisoned in the great abyss. There will be a release of these depraved demons (see Revelation 9:1–11) upon the earth, led by a powerful beast named Abaddon (in Hebrew). These soon-to-be-paroled demons have been waiting under the darkness and judgment of God for millennia to attack certain of mankind in ways that have never been experienced in the history of the world.

**CHAPTER SIX**
# The Beast Out of the Abyss

# 6

# APOLLYON:
# THE BEAST OUT OF THE ABYSS

There is another beast that Satan uses to kill, deceive, and destroy the people and the works of God. His name is Apollyon in the Greek, and Abaddon in the Hebrew. He is different from the others. He doesn't rise up out of the sea (the multitudes) nor the earth (a human), but up from the abyss—a prison for the most terrifying of demons. The abyss is a God-forsaken place of darkness, hot, thick smoke, and strange-looking demons. Some believe the abyss to be the bottomless pit; others believe it to be hell itself.

More than likely, Apollyon was one of Satan's rulers during the rebellion when one-third of the angels attempted to overthrow God and take over heaven. All these rebellious angels were thrown to the earth, thus turning them into fallen angels and demons. Many of them were not permitted to roam the earth and torment man as so many have done and still do all over the world. Many of them are much too vile and evil to be exposed to mankind. God threw them all into this abyss that is mentioned in Revelation chapter nine in order to keep them at bay.

> *And the fifth angel sounded, and I saw a star fall from heaven unto the earth; and to him was given the key of the bottomless pit. And he opened the bottomless pit; and there arose a smoke of a great furnace; and the sun and the air were darkened by reason of the smoke of the pit.* (Revelation 9:1–2)

A powerful angel (probably the Archangel Michael) is given a key to unlock the abyss, thereby releasing those demons that are imprisoned within. These demons fly like locusts; they act like horses, have the teeth of lions, have long hair like a woman, and sting like scorpions. Amazingly, they are told what they are allowed to do and what they are not allowed to do while on their short release time. Evidently, God is still restraining the demons of the abyss, because if they had the license to do as they please, they would have destroyed the earth and killed all of mankind. Revelation explains the limitations on these demons.

> *And out of the smoke locusts came down on the earth and they were given power like that of scorpions of the earth. They were told not to harm the grass of the earth or any plant or any tree, but only those people who did have not the seal of God on their foreheads. They were not allowed to kill them but only to torture them for five months. And the agony they suffered was like that of the sting of a scorpion when it strikes. During those days people will seek death but will not find it; they will long to die, but death will elude them.* (Revelation 9:3–6 RSV)

The abyss appears to be a physical place that, as some writers have suggested, is actually located in the center of the earth, rather than a dimensional place, much like heaven or hell. There have been unsubstantiated reports of groups in Europe lowering microphones down deep into the earth and recording the sound of multitudes screaming in hell. I have difficulty in this belief because of the term "bottomless" pit. The earth is just less than eight thousand miles wide, which obviously cannot be bottomless. The abyss, in turn, must be a dimension.

> *In appearance the locusts were like horses arrayed for battle; on their heads were what looked like crowns of gold; their faces were like human faces, their hair like women's hair, and their*

*teeth like lions' teeth; they had scales like iron breastplates,
and the noise of their wings was like the noise of many chariots
with horses rushing into battle. They have tails like scorpions,
and stings, and their power of hurting men for five months lies
in their tails.*                    (Revelation 9:7–10 RSV)

These locust demons have been locked up in the smoked-
filled, burning furnace of the abyss for a very long time. God
has restrained them possibly since the fall of Satan. These creatures are so vile that God has kept them on a tight leash and out
of reach of mankind. Had God not restrained and imprisoned
these creatures in an abyss, they would have filled the world with
intolerable, indiscriminate punishment and genocide. They are
so terrible; God gave them specific instructions while they were
paroled.

Arguably, these are actual, and not symbolic, demonic creatures. Many authors have written and insisted that the descriptions of these locust-type monsters are much like our helicopters of war, or fighter planes, or even modern day drones. But
I am persuaded that they are actually demonic creatures. Had
they been helicopters, fighter planes, or drones, they would
have killed people with their bombing capabilities. However,
not only do these creatures not kill anyone, their power to
inflict pain is specifically, but strangely, in their tails—like a
scorpion stinger.

This doesn't describe any of our modern day war-faring air-
crafts. Had these locust demons been weapons of man's warfare,
God would not have restrained their weaponry. One more point:
I know of no military weapon that targets grass, trees, or greenery. What helicopter aims their weapons at trees and grass? These
demonic locusts were told to leave greenery alone. Actual locusts
are attracted to greenery, but these demons are mandated specifically to inflict torment to humans only.

And strangely, the locust can only inflict their demonic stingers at those that are not marked or sealed by God. How can a military aircraft delineate between the marked and sealed people of God and the ones that are not?

**When the demon-locusts were released, they were restrained in four areas:**

+ That they could only torment man for five months.
+ That they could not destroy the grass, trees, or greenery of the earth.
+ That they could not take the life of any man.
+ And that they must not harm those that have the seal of God on their foreheads.

No one actually knows who these sealed people of God are who have been singled out not to be harmed by Apollyon. Some believe it is all of the people of God, but most disagree because they feel at this point in the timeline, the rapture has already taken place. Others feel the sealed people of God are the 144,000 Jews mentioned in Revelation 7:

> *Then I heard the number of those who were sealed: 144,000 from all the tribes of Israel.*  (Revelation 7:4 NIV)

These could very well be the sealed people mentioned Revelation 9:7–10, because, as Jews, they are possibly left behind after the rapture for the purposes of God in assisting Israel. Matthew Henry feels that the seal is indicative of the mark of the Holy Spirit, and that the Lord will not suffer His people to be afflicted by the demons. And because the seal is a spiritual mark upon the foreheads of these selected Jewish people, demons will have an aversion to them.

**The beast from the abyss: Apollyon.**

The powerful demon named Apollyon is given the power to torture any person who doesn't have the seal of God on his or her forehead. His demon locust followers have scorpion-like tails; they can torture men so intensely that they will wish to die. But death will not be granted to them. Apollyon is a ruler for Satan, with great authority and powers. Apollyon's authority and power is so intensely evil and vile that he is restrained in the abyss. However, during this Great Tribulation, he is released with great vengeance and terrifying anger.

> *They have as king over them the angel of the bottomless pit; his name in Hebrew is Abad'don, and in Greek he is called Apol'lyon.*               (Revelation 9:11 RSV)

Concerning Revelation 9:11, I can't help but notice that this terrorizing beast named Apollyon from the abyss is introduced to us in a Scripture numbered **9:11** (Revelation). The numbers 9-1-1 are emergency numbers in America and also describe the date the twin towers in New York City, were brought down by terrorists— September 11, 2001. Maybe it's a coincidence or maybe it's something God arranged to help us with signs, wonders, prophecies, and hints of His return. Either way, 9-11 will always stand for an emergency, or the date of a past disaster.

This demon leader, Apollyon or Abaddon (means destroyer), is referred to as a beast that is to come up from the abyss. An abyss is defined as a deep, immeasurable space, a gulf, a cavity, a vast chasm, a hole, a bottomless pit, an infernal region, or hell itself. Apollyon, the beast from the abyss is also mentioned in Revelation 17:8 (RSV): "*The beast that you saw was, and is not, and is to ascend from the bottomless pit.*"

In the apocryphal book of Enoch 18:12–16, Enoch says that he was taken into the actual abyss where the beast and fallen angels were imprisoned. Although the book of Enoch was not canonized, many have read the book. If you are not familiar with the book of Enoch, you might enjoy his amazing description of the abyss.

> Into the chasm I was taken, until I came to a place that did not have the heaven above it, nor the earth below it—a place of neither up nor down—a deserted and lonely place. There I saw a terrible thing, seven large burning, masses, and I questioned in my mind about this place. An angel said: This is the place between gravity above and that below– that has become the prison of the angels that have fallen. These angels here have sinned against the Lord, who like stars that would not come as commanded, so the angels who disobeyed have been imprisoned to keep them from disrupting God's plan. The Lord was angry at these fallen angels and bound them till the end times. At the end of the ages, the Lord will bring them to their final end.

I find this vivid description of the abyss quite terrifying, and though it may not be true due to the book's lack of canonization, Enoch's details are riveting to my imagination of what the actual abyss could be.

John D. Ladd, who wrote an extraordinary commentary on the books of Enoch, said that Enoch shared the name of the beast that comes out of the abyss, and that he is also called *Belial*, from the Hebrew meaning a being of no ascent or resurrection. Enoch continues and tells the reader that the beast from the abyss is also named *Metanbuchus*, which is from the two Hebrew words *"mattan bukah,"* meaning the gift of the abyss. Enoch described this beast as being part human and part fallen, angelic spirit. He said that during the Tower of Babel, Beliel was the evil spirit that stood as a false god who was served by many people in those times directly after the flood.

He has since been imprisoned in the abyss. Some commentaries share that Apollyon, who had many names, was actually worshipped as the false god Apollo. Many Greeks and Romans worshipped Apollo as the greatest of all the gods—even more powerful than Zeus, Thor, Hades, and Poseidon. Many of the fallen angels, and demons, have poised themselves before mankind as gods to be worshipped, thereby turning people from the one true God. Men have committed abominations, sacrificed animals and humans, worshipped and praised these false gods, and denied the God of Abraham, Isaac, and Jacob.

In Enoch 10:1–9, Enoch mentions how and when the beast was thrown into the abyss:

> Then said the Most High, the Holy and Great One spake, and sent Uriel (angel of God) to the son of Lamech [Noah], and said to him, God of Noah and tell him in my Name, "Hide thyself!" And reveal to him the end is approaching: that the whole earth will be destroyed, and a deluge is about to come upon the whole earth, and will destroy all that is on it. And so instruct him that he may escape and his seed may be preserved for all generations of the world. And again the Lord said to Raphael: bind Azazel (Apollyon) hand and foot, and cast him into darkness, and make an opening in the desert...and cast him there in. And place upon him rough and jagged rocks, and cover him with darkness, and let him abide there forever, and cover his face that he may not see light. And on the day of the great judgment he shall be cast into fire. And heal the earth in which the angels have corrupted, and proclaim healing of the earth, that they may heal the plague.

**The beast from out of the abyss (Apollyon) will be given power to kill the two witnesses of God.**

Though Apollyon's locust-like, demon followers are not permitted to kill man, there is one exception. Sadly, Apollyon will be permitted to kill the two witnesses mentioned in Revelation chapter eleven. I realize that the following Scriptures provided below are a bit lengthy; however, it is the story of the two witnesses as told by John:

> And I will appoint my two witnesses, and they will prophesy for 1,260 days, clothed in sackcloth. They are "the two olive trees" and the two lampstands, and "they stand before the Lord of the earth." If anyone tries to harm them, fire comes from their mouths and devours their enemies. This is how anyone who wants to harm them must die. They have power to shut up the heavens so that it will not rain during the time they are prophesying; and they have power to turn the waters into blood and to strike the earth with every kind of plague as often as they want. Now when they [two witnesses] have finished their testimony, **the beast that comes up out of the abyss will attack them, and overpower and kill them.** Their bodies will lie in the public square of the great city—which is figuratively called Sodom and Egypt—where also their Lord was crucified. For three and a half days some from every people, tribe, language and nation will gaze on their dead bodies for three and a half days and refuse them burial. The inhabitants of the earth will gloat over them and will celebrate by sending each other gifts, because these two prophets had tormented those who live on the earth. But after three and a half days the breath of life from God entered them, and they stood on their feet, and terror struck those who saw them. . Then they heard a loud voice from heaven saying to them, "Come up here." And they went up to heaven in a cloud, while their enemies looked on. At that very hour there was a severe earthquake and a tenth of the city collapsed. Seven thousand people were

*killed in the earthquake, and the survivors were terrified and gave glory to the God of heaven.* (Revelation 11:3–13 NIV)

The two witnesses will be such a torment to the people of Jerusalem (probably a torment to Islam), that they will attack the prophets in order to kill them. The Bible says that the witnesses will open their mouths and fire will come out to kill their enemies. More than likely, the fire is a depiction of their fiery words that curse their opponents, which instantly kills them. They also have the power of Moses to turn water into blood, and the power of Elijah to stop the rain from falling for three and half years. It is believed by some commentators that these two witnesses are actually Moses and Elijah returned to the earth.

Once the two witnesses are finished with their testimonies, prophecies, and preaching, God gives Apollyon the power to kill the two of them. Once they are declared dead (people will be so full of hatred toward the true God, His Word, and His prophesies, that they will want to kill these two prophets), people will celebrate and rejoice over their deaths even though Satan through Apollyon kill them.

Amazingly, after the two witnesses are assassinated in the middle of the street, the world celebrates their deaths while their dead bodies lie there for three and a half days in the hot sun of Jerusalem. The deaths of the two witnesses are such a huge relief to these worldly people (probably Islam), that they send each other presents to commemorate the day they died. These witnesses are described as tormenting the people—evidently with prophecies and the Word of God.

I surmise that they are preaching about Jesus Christ being the only begotten Son of God, that He came from heaven, and was crucified, and rose again the third day. I would not doubt that these two witnesses will be openly opposing Islam, sharia law, Muslimism, the papal, worldwide religion, the Antichrist, the false prophet, doctrines of men and devils, and possibly warning of them of Second Coming of Christ.

Apollyon, the other beasts, the whore, false religion, the Antichrist, the false prophet, and evil in general will be defeated by the soon coming of a very determined and angry Son of God. He will return with a terrible vengeance to avenge those who were martyred for His name's sake, to mete out judgment upon Satan, the false prophet, and Antichrist. His face will not be the same as what the twelve apostles saw while Jesus walked the earth during His ministry. He will have a fierce countenance, with flames of fire, white hair like wool, and a double-edged sword protruding out of His mouth to indicate His words defeating His enemies. Where once he entered Jerusalem on a peaceful donkey, He will return on a white warhorse. He will bring immediate victory over all of the beasts. And He is the only one that has the ability to do so.

# Conclusion

# CONCLUSION

In the end, the unified efforts of the five beasts from the sea, land, abyss, the crimson beast, the dragon (all of which are empowered by Satan), will ravage the world, killing indiscriminately all those who do not adhere to the Islamic doctrine of devils and sharia law. This satanic, unified effort will culminate at the valley of Jezreel for the ultimate battle of Armageddon, where the depth of spilled blood of the fallen soldiers will be measured, not in inches, but in feet and length of miles. Nations will fall to these beasts, oppositional politics will cease to a one-world government, and religions will cease to a one-world religion—all of which will be under the blood-soaked banner of radical Islam. True Christians and Jews will be the focal point of Islamic jihads. In other words, Islam will be intent to erase the Jews and Christians off the face of the earth, more quickly and aggressively than Islam is attacking Jews and Christians right now.

The peripheral partners of this unification effort will be the Vatican, the pope and his Holy See, One World Council of Churches (or false Christianity), the United Nations, the unified Arab-Islamic national efforts, and, of course, literal demons that will run rampart through the earth, afflicting man without mercy. Before it eventually turns on itself, this unified effort, will invade Israel. Damascus will be a literal ruinous heap, and conventional and nuclear warfare will decimate multitudes.

This book did not cover the efforts of Gog and Magog's (Russia—probably similar to communist USSR once again) intentions of world domination, and of course the two hundred million-man Chinese army that will invade the Middle East to make war as well to ensure their interests there.

There are also the terrible acts of God, by way of opening seals and the sounding of trumpets, that will send eruptions of violent events of nature like earthquakes, droughts, sun burning skin off of men's backs, *and the earth will reel to and fro like a drunken man*— setting off devastating reactions that will affect agriculture worldwide. Poverty, hunger, thirst, fear gripping men's hearts, signs in the sun, moon, and stars, falling comets, meteorites, and asteroids crashing into the earth, just to name a few.

Among the radical Islamic nations, Iran is the tip of the spear in this unified effort to present the Antichrist and false prophet to the world. The Islamic religious leaders, according to the Hadith, say that as soon as Islam invades Israel, the Mahdi will reveal himself on a white horse, proclaiming Islam as sovereign. Christians and Jews must be eradicated, and the entire world must recognize Islam as the sovereign religion.

Those who convert to Islam and show their allegiance to Islam must not only worship Islam's deity, but also must worship Islam's image or symbol, and receive Islam's mark (mark of the beast). Sadly, all of those who give their allegiance and convert to Islam and receive Islam's mark of the beast will be condemned by God's judgment. I realize that this is not a universal belief and that other commentaries state that the mark of the beast will be a European, financial mark, but I stand in the belief that God will judge those who recant Christ by choosing Allah and Islam. I do not believe that God will punish mankind for receiving a mark for strictly financial reasons, like an injected capsule with filled with information of one's identity. The mark must be a representation of one's choosing of a false god, an open denouncement of Jesus Christ, and a worship of an image.

When the appointed time has struck, God will send His Son, with all the saints behind Him, and bring all of His enemies to their end. I believe that the Second Coming and the Rapture or resurrection of the saints are simultaneous, in that we, as the children of God shall be caught up to meet Jesus in the air, then return to the earth with Him as He rides upon His white warhorse. His feet will lighten upon Mount Olivet and it will part in two as an earthquake.

Jesus then will enter into the old city of Jerusalem through the Eastern Gate. Humorously, the radical Muslims have blocked up the present Eastern Gate, and laid a gravesite up against it in order to block any possibility of Jesus entering into the city via the Eastern Gate. It is their belief that Jesus, a priest, by Hebrew law cannot touch the dead or anything that touches the dead such as a gravesite. All of this is absolutely ridiculous, except, I find it curious that Islamists took precautions in case Jesus does actually appear according to the Old Testament prophecies and the proclamation of the angel to the disciples while Jesus ascended into heaven.

At the conclusion of the battle, Satan, the Antichrist, and the false prophet will be cast into the bottomless pit. This will put an end to all of the beasts, and an end to the source of evil upon the earth. The Millennial Age will be set up upon the earth with Jesus literally sitting upon the earth, ruling with a rod of iron—meaning He will not tolerate wickedness and evil for His thousand-year reign. Mankind will return to living very long lives of hundreds of years old. Seemingly, no beast or man will be carnivorous during this age, and the fruit from the trees will have incredible ability to keep men healthy.

After the thousand years have transpired, Satan will be released for a short season to deceive and terrorize the nations once again, and Gog and Magog (Russia) will be used one last time by Satan as a war beast that will wage war against mankind. Then the final judgment will come – the White Throne Judgment of God. This is when hell itself, and all of the wicked of the world, will be cast into the Lake of Fire along with Satan.

Let me encourage you, if you are not a believer in Jesus Christ, to give your life to Him immediately. Jesus Christ loves you so much and does not want you to perish, but to be with Him in heaven for all eternity. You must know that His love for you drove Him to the cross to die for you. It is important to your salvation to proclaim Jesus as the only Savior of the world, and the only way to God and heaven. True Christianity cannot make room for other saviors, other routes to heaven, and ways to God Almighty outside of Jesus Christ, His only begotten Son. This is pertinent, because the world would have you to believe that you need an open mind to other religions and other saviors. This thinking is the spirit of antichrist.

Jesus is not just another option for man to choose from, He is the only option to choose from.

Choose Jesus today, and you will live with Him for all eternity!

CPSIA information can be obtained at www.ICGtesting.com
Printed in the USA
LVOW04s0622030215

425469LV00005B/52/P